Everyday Mathematics®

Study Links

Everyday Mathematics®

Study Links

The University of Chicago
School Mathematics Project

A Division of The McGraw·Hill Companies

Columbus, Ohio
Chicago, Illinois

UCSMP Elementary Materials Component
Max Bell, Director

Authors
Max Bell
John Bretzlauf
Amy Dillard
Robert Hartfield
Andy Isaacs

James McBride, Director
Kathleen Pitvorec
Peter Saecker
Robert Balfanz*
William Carroll*

Technical Art
Diana Barrie*

*First Edition only

Photo Credits
Phil Martin/Photography

This material is based upon work supported by the National Science Foundation under Grant No. ESI-9252984. Any opinions, findings, and conclusions or recommendations expressed in this material are those of the authors and do not necessarily reflect the views of the National Science Foundation.

www.sra4kids.com

SRA/McGraw-Hill
A Division of The McGraw-Hill Companies

Send all inquiries to:
SRA/McGraw-Hill
P.O. Box 812960
Chicago, IL 60681

Printed in the United States of America.

ISBN 1-57039-974-3

12 13 14 15 MAL 09 08 07 06

Contents

Family Letter

Introduction to Sixth Grade Everyday Mathematics®

The mathematics program we are using this year—*Everyday Mathematics*—offers students a broad background in mathematics. Some approaches in this program may differ from those you used as a student. However, they are based on research results, field-test experiences, and the mathematics that students will need in the 21st century. Following are some program highlights:

- A problem-solving approach that uses mathematics in everyday situations

- A balance of independent activities that develop confidence and self-reliance, as well as partner and small-group activities that promote cooperative learning

- Concepts and skills introduced and reviewed throughout the school year, promoting retention through a variety of exposures

- Concepts and skills developed through hands-on activities

- Opportunities to discuss and communicate mathematically

- Frequent practice using games as alternatives to tedious drills

- Opportunities for home and school communication

Sixth Grade Everyday Mathematics emphasizes the following content:

Numbers, Numeration, Equivalence, and Order Relations Recognizing place value in numerals for whole numbers and decimals; expressing numbers in scientific notation; finding factors of numbers; representing rates and ratios with fraction notation; finding equivalent fractions; using ratios to describe size change.

Measurement, Measures, and Numbers in Reference Frames Using linear, area, capacity, and personal reference measures; using metric and U.S. customary units.

Operations, Mental Arithmetic, and Number Systems Performing addition, subtraction, multiplication, and division of whole numbers, fractions, and decimals; evaluating symbolic expressions; applying the distributive property.

Algorithms and Procedures Reviewing multiplication and division algorithms for whole numbers; developing algorithms for operations on positive and negative rational numbers.

Problem Solving and Mathematical Modeling Using probability; using strategies for multiple-choice tests; analyzing games of chance; exploring trial-and-error methods, maze problems, mobile problems, and maximum-minimum problems.

Exploring Data Collecting, organizing, and analyzing data using line plots, bar graphs, line graphs, circle graphs, and step graphs; interpreting persuasive graphs and mystery graphs; identifying landmarks of data sets (median, mean, mode, and range).

Geometry and Spatial Sense Measuring and drawing angles; investigating angles of rotation; making compass-and-straightedge constructions; drawing to scale; exploring how transformations affect attributes of geometric shapes; experimenting with tessellations, topology (rubber-sheet geometry), and Möbius strips.

Patterns, Rules, and Formulas Applying formulas to geometric figures; using variables in formulas; working with Venn diagrams and tree diagrams; solving pan-balance problems.

Algebra and Uses of Variables Creating number models; working with scientific calculators; exploring variables in formulas; simplifying algebraic expressions; solving equations and inequalities.

Throughout the year, you will receive Family Letters telling you about the mathematical content to be studied in each unit. Letters may include definitions of new terms, as well as suggestions for at-home activities designed to reinforce skills. We are looking forward to an exciting year filled with discovery. You will enjoy seeing your child's mathematical understanding grow.

Building Skills through Games

In this unit, your child will work on his or her understanding of estimation, measurement, and fractions by playing the following games. For more detailed instructions, see the *Student Reference Book*.

Name That Number See *Student Reference Book,* page 301
This games provides the student with practice in naming numbers with equivalent expressions. Two or three players need 1 complete deck of number cards to play *Name That Number.*

Landmark Shark See *Student Reference Book,* pages 299 and 300
Two or three players use 1 complete deck of number cards, 1 range, median, and mode card for each player, and a score sheet to play *Landmark Shark.* This game affords the student practice with finding the range, mode, median, and mean of a set of numbers.

Use with Lesson 1.1.

Unit 1: Collection, Display, and Interpretation of Data

Everyday Mathematics will help your child use mathematics effectively in daily life. For example, the media—especially newspapers and magazines—use data. Employees and employers need to know how to gather, analyze, and display data in order to work efficiently. Consumers need to know how to interpret and question the data that are presented to them in order to make informed choices. Citizens need to understand the government data in order to participate in the running of their country.

In *Everyday Mathematics,* data provide a context for the development of numerical skills that, in traditional programs, would be developed artificially or in isolation. In Unit 1, your child will work with data displayed in bar graphs, circle graphs, step graphs, broken-line graphs, and tables.

Bar graph

Circle graph

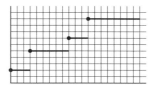

Step graph

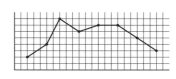

Line graph

These displays relate to such topics as temperature, postal rates, wages, and the type of crust preferred by pizza eaters, to name just a few. These real-world applications support and enrich other areas of mathematics as well.

Throughout Unit 1, your child will be encouraged to look for graphs and tables in newspapers and magazines and to bring them to school (after getting permission). The class will be asked to think critically about the materials collected. For example, students will consider the following questions:

- What is the purpose of the graph or table?

- Is the display clear? Attractive? Can it be improved?

- Does the display seem accurate, or is it biased?

- Can you draw any conclusions from or make any predictions based on the information in this graph or table?

Finally, students will learn a new game, *Landmark Shark,* which will help them develop skill in finding the landmarks of data in various data sets. Ask your child to teach you how to play this game.

This should be a stimulating year, and we invite you to share the excitement with us!

Please keep this Family Letter for reference as your child works through Unit 1.

As You Help Your Child with Homework

As your child brings assignments home, you may want to go over the instructions together, clarifying them as necessary. The answers listed below will guide you through this unit's Study Links.

Study Link 1.2

2. 90   **3.** 0   **4.** 6   **5.** 6   **6.** B

Study Link 1.3

1. Alicia _75_   Blanca _75_

3. Nearly the same   **4.** Nearly the same

5. Sample answer: The median and mean scores are similar for both students. However, the range of Blanca's scores is much larger than the range of Alicia's scores.

6. Sample answer: Alicia's scores are more consistent. Blanca scored very well on two tests but did poorly on others. We need more information to decide who is a better student.

Study Link 1.4

1. a. 131   **b.** 169   **c.** 147.5   **d.** 149.2

2. a. 138   **b.** 167   **c.** 149   **d.** 151.3

Study Link 1.5

1.

Elapsed Time (minutes)	Temperature (°F)
0 (pour tea)	160
10	120
40	85
20	100
12.5	115
5	140

2. 90 °F   **3.** About 25 min

4. a. Sample answer: About 100 min

   b. Sample answer: The rate of cooling seems to level off to $2\frac{1}{2}$°F every 10 minutes.

5. a. no

   b. Sample answer: The tea cools off very quickly at first; but after awhile, the temperature drops slowly.

Study Link 1.6

2. 5   **3.** 2   **4.** 3 times

5. 2 times   **6.** 2, 3   **7.** 4

Study Link 1.7

2. $1.21   **3. a.** $1.65

Study Link 1.8

2. men   **3. a.** 89%   **b.** 11%

4. 10% greater   **5.** 60% greater

Study Link 1.9

1. a. 94 ft   **b.** 288 ft   **c.** 50 ft   **d.** 4,700 ft^2

2. a. 27 cm   **b.** 21 cm^2 **3.** 37.7 ft

Study Link 1.10

1. a. About 58 minutes

   b. Sample answer: I divided 9.5 billion by the number of working adults, 163,000,000. The answer was 58.2822..., so I rounded it off to 58.

2. a. 0.05, 0.04

   b. Sample answer: I divided 40 by the number of years a person lives to find out how many pounds per year are shed (0.543 for men, 0.505 for women). Then I divided each by 12 months to find out how much is shed each month and rounded off each answer to the nearest hundredth.

Study Link 1.11

1. 640   **2.** 150   **3.** 80

4. 40   **5.** 10,800

Mystery Line Plots and Landmarks

1. Draw a line plot for the following spelling test scores.
100, 100, 95, 90, 92, 93, 96, 90, 94, 90, 97

```
_____
   90   91   92   93   94   95   96   97   98   99   100
```

2. The mode of the above data is _____.

Mr. Martinez surveyed his health class. He asked the following questions:

   A. About how many hours do you sleep each night?

   B. About how many glasses of milk do you drink per day?

   C. What is your heart rate in beats per minute after exercising for one minute?

Tomás sketched a line plot (see below) of the class results for one of the questions, but he forgot to label his line plot.

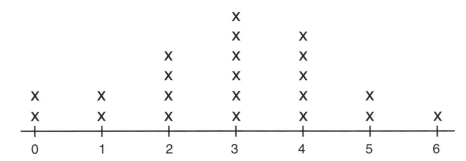

3. The **minimum** of the data is _____.

4. The **maximum** of the data is _____.

5. The **range** of the data is _____.

6. Which of the questions do you think is represented by his line plot? _____

   Explain your reasoning.

   _____

   _____

Median and Mean

Alicia's quiz scores are 75, 75, 70, 80, and 75.
Blanca's quiz scores are 50, 70, 90, 100, and 65.

1. Find each girl's mean (or average) score.

Alicia _____   Blanca _____

2. Use the number lines below to make one line plot for Alicia's scores and a
second line plot for Blanca's scores.

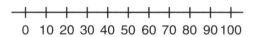

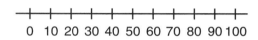

        a. Alicia's Scores   **b.** Blanca's Scores

3. Is Alicia's median score the same, or
nearly the same, as Blanca's median score? _____

4. Are the girls' median scores the same,
or nearly the same, as their mean scores? _____

5. In which ways are Alicia's and Blanca's scores similar?
In which ways are their scores different? Explain.

_____

_____

_____

_____

6. Who do you think might be the better student? Explain.

_____

_____

_____

_____

_____

Minimum, Maximum, Median, and Mean

Heights were measured to the nearest centimeter for 12 boys and 12 girls. All of the boys and girls were 12 years old.

Boys' heights: 157, 150, 131, 143, 147, 169, 148, 147, 145, 163, 139, 151

Girls' heights: 146, 164, 138, 149, 145, 167, 150, 156, 143, 148, 149, 160

1. Make a line plot for the boys' data. Then find the minimum, maximum, median, and mean of the boys' heights.

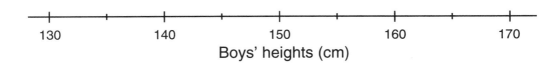

Boys' heights (cm)

a. minimum _____   **b.** maximum _____

c. median _____   **d.** mean _____

2. Make a line plot for the girls' data. Then find the minimum, maximum, median, and mean of the girls' heights.

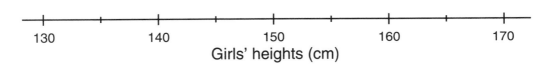

Girls' heights (cm)

a. minimum _____   **b.** maximum _____

c. median _____   **d.** mean _____

---

3. Do people prefer big numbers or small numbers? *Predict:* If you were to ask three people to name a number between 0 and 100, what results would you be likely to get?

_____

4. Ask three people to name a number between 0 and 100. Record the results.

Person 1 _____   Person 2 _____   Person 3 _____

During your next math class, you will use your data, along with your classmates' data, to check your prediction.

Cooling Off

The graph below shows how a cup of hot
tea cools as time passes.

1. Use the graph below to fill in the missing
data in the table on the right.

2. What is the approximate temperature
of the tea after 30 minutes?

_____

3. About how many minutes does it take
for the tea to cool to a temperature
of 95°F?

_____

Elapsed Time (minutes)	Temperature (°F)
0 (pour tea)	
10	
40	
	100
	115
5	

4. **a.** About how many minutes do you
think it will take the tea to cool to
room temperature?

_____

_____

b. Why do you think so?

_____

_____

_____

_____

5. **a.** Does the tea cool at a constant rate?

_____

b. Explain your answer. _____

_____

_____

Using Bar Graphs

Every week, Ms. Penczar gives a math quiz to her class of 15 students. The table at the right shows the class's average scores for a six-week period.

1. Draw a bar graph that shows the same information. Be sure to give the graph a title and to label each axis.

Use the bar graph you just drew to answer the following questions.

Week	Class Average
1	68
2	66
3	79
4	89
5	91
6	88

2. The highest average score occurred in

Week _____.

3. The lowest average score occurred in

Week _____.

4. How many times was there an improvement from one week to the next?

_____

5. How many times was there a decline from one week to the next?

_____

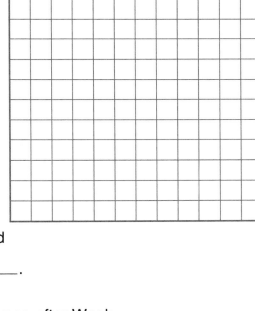

6. The greatest one-week improvement occurred

between Week _____ and Week _____.

7. There was little improvement in the class average after Week _____.

8. Name a possible set of scores for Ms. Penczar's 15 students that would result in the class average given for Week 2.

_____ _____ _____ _____ _____

_____ _____ _____ _____ _____

_____ _____ _____ _____ _____

The Cost of Mailing a Letter

In the United States, the cost of mailing a first-class letter depends on how much the letter weighs. The table at the right shows first-class postal rates in 2000: 33 cents for a letter weighing 1 ounce or less; 55 cents for a letter weighing more than 1 ounce but not more than 2 ounces; and so on.

Weight (oz)	Cost
1	$0.33
2	$0.55
3	$0.77
4	$0.99
5	$1.21
6	$1.43

A step graph for these data has been started on the next page. Notice the placement of dots in the graph. For example, on the step representing 55 cents, the dot at the right end, above the 2, shows that it costs 55 cents to mail a letter weighing exactly 2 ounces. There is no dot at the left end of the step—that is, at the intersection of 1 ounce and 55 cents—because the cost of mailing a 1-ounce letter is 33 cents, not 55 cents.

1. Continue the graph for letters weighing up to 6 ounces.

2. At these rates, how much would it cost to send a letter that weighs $4\frac{1}{2}$ ounces? _____

Challenge

3. a. At these rates, how much would it cost to mail a letter that weighs $6\frac{1}{2}$ ounces? _____

    b. How did you determine your answer?

    _____

    _____

    _____

4. Continue the graph to show the cost of mailing a first-class letter weighing more than 6 ounces but not more than 7 ounces.

The Cost of Mailing a Letter (cont.)

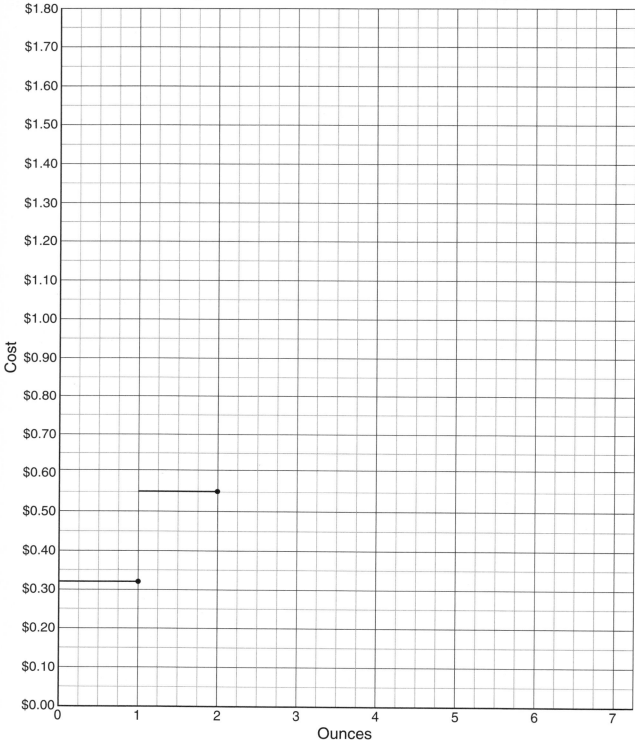

Cost of Mailing a First-Class Letter in the United States in 2000

Use with Lesson 1.7.

Analyzing Circle Graphs

1. Would you be willing to tell strangers that they had

smudges on their faces?   yes   no

food stuck between their teeth?   yes   no

dandruff?   yes   no

A marketing research company asked men and women these very questions.
The results are summarized in the circle graphs below.

Use the legend to read the graphs.

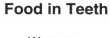 yes, will tell   no, will not tell

Smudge on Face	**Food in Teeth**	**Dandruff**
Women	Women	Women
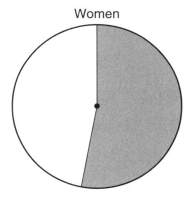	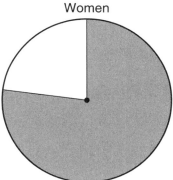	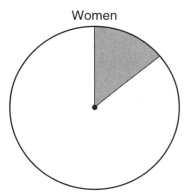
Men	Men	Men
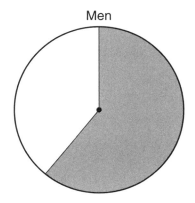	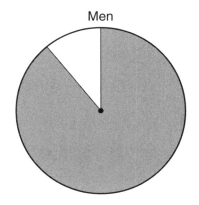	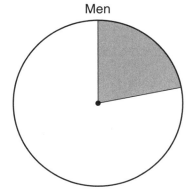

Source: America by the Numbers

Analyzing Circle Graphs (cont.)

Cut out the Percent Circle on the bottom of this page, and poke a hole in the center with a pencil. Use the Percent Circle to find what percent of the graphs the sectors represent when you answer the questions below.

2. According to the survey, are men or women more likely to alert strangers to an embarrassing situation? _____

3. **a.** About what percent of *men* say they would tell strangers that they had food stuck between their teeth? _____

    b. About what percent of men would not be willing to tell? _____

4. In the survey, how much greater is the percent of *men* who would be willing to alert strangers to smudges on their faces than the percent of *women* who would be willing to do so? _____

5. How much greater is the percent of women who would be willing to tell strangers about food in their teeth than the percent of women who would tell strangers about their dandruff? _____

6. Why do you suppose men and women might be hesitant to alert strangers to such situations?

    _____

    _____

    _____

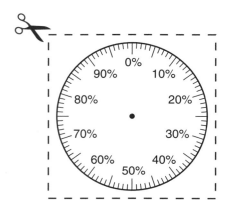

Perimeter and Area in Basketball

Be sure to include the unit of measure in each of your answers.

1. The following diagram shows the dimensions of a basketball court.

   Hint: To find the length of the court, first find the length of the right half-court.

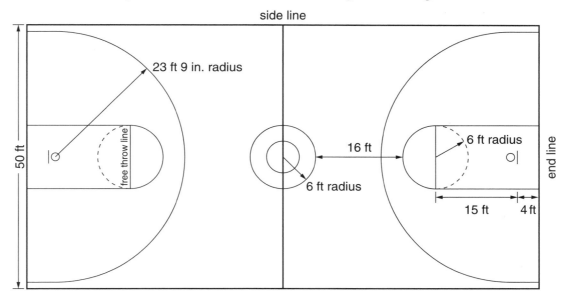

   a. What is the length of the court? _____   **b.** What is its perimeter? _____

   c. What is its width? _____   **d.** What is its area? _____

2. Measure the sides of polygon *ABSOLUTELY* with a centimeter ruler. Write the length on each side.

   Hint: To find the area, divide the interior of the polygon into rectangular regions.

   a. What is its perimeter? _____

   b. What is its area? _____

Challenge

3. What is the "perimeter" (circumference) of the larger circle at the center of the basketball court?

   _____

Statistics Meant to Astound

Sometimes statistics are reported colorfully in newspapers in an attempt to astound or influence readers. Use the information provided below to make the statistics sound less astounding.

1. In the United States, people spend about 9.5 billion minutes on the telephone during an average business day. In 1997, the estimated population in the United States of people between the ages of 19 and 64 was about 163,000,000.

    a. About how many minutes per day does the average person between the ages of 19 and 64 spend on the telephone?

    About _____ minutes

    b. Describe the strategy you used to solve the problem.

    _____

    _____

    _____

2. During an average lifetime, a person sheds about 40 pounds of dead skin. In the United States, life expectancy for men is about 73.6 years. Life expectancy for women is about 79.2 years.

    a. A man would shed about _____ pounds of dead skin in a month.

    A woman would shed about _____ pounds of dead skin in a month.

    b. Describe the strategy you used to solve the problem.

    _____

    _____

    _____

    _____

    _____

    _____

Kitchen Units of Capacity

Solve.

1. Find the number of quarts in 4 gallons.

Multiply by 20. Double that. _____

2. Find the number of pints in 5 quarts.

Multiply by 30. Divide by 2. _____

3. Find the number of cups in 2 gallons. Multiply by 200. Divide by 80. _____

4. Find the number of pints in 70 gallons. Divide by 2. Divide by 7. _____

5. Find the number of cups in 10 quarts. Multiply by 90. Triple that. _____

Write three problems about kitchen measures to share with the class.

6. _____

_____

_____

_____

_____

7. _____

_____

_____

_____

_____

8. _____

_____

_____

_____

_____

Family Letter

Unit 2: Rational Number Uses and Operations

In Unit 2, your child will revisit operations with whole numbers and decimals and will extend previously developed skills. We will look at estimation strategies, mental methods, pencil-and-paper algorithms, and calculator procedures. We will develop techniques for placing the decimal point in answers.

Also in Unit 2, we will see how to represent very large and very small numbers with number-and-word notation, exponential notation, and scientific notation.

Many of the numbers used to express measures, such as distances of planets from the Sun, are so large that they become cumbersome to write and difficult to understand. For example, the distance from the Sun to the planet Pluto might be given as 3,675,000,000 (three billion, six hundred seventy-five million) miles. Similarly, distances within atoms are extremely small.

Your child will learn that scientific notation is one way that mathematicians and scientists express very large and very small numbers. In scientific notation, the above number would be written as $3.675 * 10^9$.

In order to use scientific notation, your child will first need to know about exponential notation, which is a way of representing repeated multiplication. For example, $7 * 7 * 7 * 7$ can be written as 7^4. Similarly, since 100,000 is equal to $10 * 10 * 10 * 10 * 10$, it can be written in exponential notation as 10^5. For practice with exponential notation, students will play the game *Exponent Ball*. The rules are on page 287 of the *Student Reference Book*.

Unit 2 ends with a review of the partial quotients algorithm, which students used in *Fourth* and *Fifth Grade Everyday Mathematics* to divide whole numbers. This algorithm is extended to division of decimals by whole numbers, and students learn how to express the quotient of two whole numbers as a decimal.

The partial quotients algorithm is similar to the traditional "long division" algorithm taught for many years in the United States, but it has the advantage that it is easier to learn and apply. The quotient is built up in easy steps; the student doesn't have to get the partial quotient exactly right at each step, and can use "easy" multiples of the divisor.

Example

```
12)3270
 −2400 │ 200      First partial quotient. 200 * 12 = 2400
   870 │          Subtract. 870 is left to divide.
 − 600 │  50      Second partial quotient. 50 * 12 = 600
   270 │          Subtract. 270 is left.
 − 240 │  20      Third partial quotient. 20 * 12 = 240
    30 │          Subtract. 30 is left.
 −  24 │   2      Fourth partial quotient. 2 * 12 = 24
     6   272      Subtract. Then add the partial quotients.
     ↑    ↑
 Remainder  Quotient
```

The partial quotients algorithm is discussed on pages 22–24 of the *Student Reference Book*.

Please keep this Family Letter for reference as your child works through Unit 2.

Vocabulary

Important terms in Unit 2:

dividend In division, the number that is being divided. For example, in 35 ÷ 5 = 7, the dividend is 35.

dividend / divisor = quotient

$\frac{dividend}{divisor}$ = quotient

divisor In division, the number that divides another number. For example, in 35 ÷ 5 = 7, the divisor is 5.

exponent A small, raised number in *exponential notation* that tells how many times the base is to be multiplied by itself. For example, in 5^3, the exponent is 3.

exponential notation A way to show repeated multiplication by the same factor. For example, 2^3 is exponential notation for 2 * 2 * 2. The small, raised 3 is the exponent. It tells how many times the number 2, called the base, is used as a factor.

factor One of two or more numbers that are multiplied to give a product. The numbers that are multiplied are called *factors* of the product. For example, 4 and 3 are factors of 12 because 4 * 3 = 12. *Factor* can also mean to find two (or more) smaller numbers whose product equals a given number. 15, for example, can be factored as 5 * 3.

number-and-word notation A way of writing a large number using a combination of numbers and words. For example, 27 billion is number-and-word notation for 27,000,000,000.

power A product of factors that are all the same. For example, 5 * 5 * 5 (or 125) is called "5 to the third power" or "the third power of 5," because 5 is a factor three times.

power of 10 A whole number that can be written using only 10s as a factors. For example 100 is equal to 10 * 10, or 10^2.

powers key The ⌃ key on a calculator, used to calculate powers. Keying in 4 ⌃ 5 gives the fifth power of 4 , or 4^5, which equals 1024.

precision A description of the exactness of a measurement. The smaller the unit or fraction of a unit used, the more precise the measurement or scale. For example, a measurement to the nearest inch is more precise than a measurement to the nearest foot.

quotient The result of dividing one number by another number. For example, in 35 ÷ 5 = 7, the quotient is 7.

remainder An amount left over when one number is divided by another number. For example, if you divide 38 by 5, you get 7 equal groups with remainder 3. We may write 38 ÷ 5 → 7 R3, where R3 stands for the remainder.

scientific notation A system for writing numbers in which a number is written as the product of a *power of 10* and a number that is at least 1 and less than 10. Scientific notation allows you to write big and small numbers with only a few symbols. For example, $4 * 10^{12}$ is scientific notation for 4,000,000,000,000.

standard notation The most familiar way of representing whole numbers, integers, and decimals. In standard notation, the value of each digit depends on where the digit is in the number. For example, standard notation for three hundred fifty-six is 356.

Use with Lesson 1.12.

Do-Anytime Activities

To work with your child on the concepts taught in this unit, try these interesting and rewarding activities:

1 Encourage your child to recognize the everyday uses of fractions and decimals in fields such as science, statistics, business, sports, print and television journalism, and so on.

2 Encourage your child to incorporate the vocabulary of fractions and decimals into their everyday speech. Make sure they understand that "one-tenth" is equivalent to "10%," "one-quarter" to "25%," "three-quarters" to "75%," and so on.

3 If you are planning a dinner party or a big meal, have your child help you adjust the amounts of each ingredient needed to be proportionally correct.

4 Have your child calculate the tip of a restaurant bill through mental math and estimation. For example, if the bill is $25.00 and you intend to tip 15%, have your child go through the following mental algorithm: "10% of $25.00 is $2.50. Half of $2.50 (5%) is $1.25. $2.50 (10%) + $1.25 (5%) would be a tip of $3.75 (15%). The total amount to leave on the table would be $28.75."

Building Skills through Games

In Unit 2, your child will study the uses of fractions and rational numbers by playing the following games. For detailed instructions, please refer to the *Student Reference Book.*

Division Dash See *Student Reference Book,* page 284
Division Dash helps students practice division with 1-digit numbers. One or two players try to reach 100 on a calculator in as few divisions as possible.

Doggone Decimal See *Student Reference Book,* page 285
Two players compete to collect the most number cards. This game provides practice in estimating products of whole numbers and decimals.

Exponent Ball See *Student Reference Book,* page 287
Two players will need an *Exponent Ball* gameboard, 1 six-sided die, a penny or other counter, and a calculator to play this game. *Exponent Ball* provides students with practice in exponential notation in the context of a game similar to U.S. football.

As You Help Your Child with Homework

As your child brings assignments home, you may want to go over the instructions together, clarifying them as necessary. The answers listed below will guide you through this unit's Study Links.

Study Link 2.1

1. .11 minutes faster
2. 1.339 mph faster
3. 1.38 goals
4. 5.81 meters longer
5. 169.137
6. 4.572
7. 536.5
8. 1.541

Study Link 2.2

1. 2,001
2. 1,288
3. 11,904
4. 20.01
5. 20.01
6. 200.1
7. 250
8. 40
9. 90
10. 1
11. 5,000
12. 53.8238
13. 964.08
14. 40.071
15. 0.2826

Study Link 2.3

6. 16.32
7. 53.36
8. 18.012
9. 29.82
10. 49.92
11. 44.84
12. 76.7 miles; 11.8 * 6.5 = 76.7
13. 13.75 pages; $(1.25 \times 4) \times 2.75 = 13.75$; or $1.25 \times 11 = 13.75$
14. 4.06 square meters; $1.4 \times 2.9 = 4.06$

Study Link 2.4

1. 0.0049
2. 0.078
3. 70
4. 0.8
5. 3
6. 0.7
7. 150
8. 190
9c. 0.8

Study Link 2.5

1. 3,700,000
3. 44,300,000,000
5. 700,000,000,000
7. 4.6 million
10. Sample answer: 1 billion cards divided by 275 million people is about 4 cards for every person in the United States. That is reasonable.
11. Sample answer: That's about 2 servings per day, per person. That number is reasonable.

Study Link 2.6

1. 38.469
2. 1.3406
3. eight tenths
4. ninety-five hundredths
5. five hundredths
6. sixty-seven thousandths
7. four and eight hundred two ten-thousandths
8. hundred-thousandths
9. thousandths
10. thousandths, thousandths

Study Link 2.7

1. 49
2. 0.0625
3. 64
4. 0.068921
5. 0.00001
6. 0.015625
7. 3^9
8. 8^7
9. 4^{-3}
10. 0.5^{-6}
11. 3 * 3 * 3 * 3
12. 4 * 4 * 4 * 4 * 4 * 4
13. 0.1 * 0.1
14. 0.1 * 0.1 * 0.1 * 0.1 * 0.1
15. <u>Exponential notation</u> is a shorthand way to write products of repeated <u>factors</u>. The factor is called the <u>base</u>. The number of times it is repeated is indicated by the <u>exponent</u>.

Study Link 2.8

1. 30,000,000
3. 6,000,000
5. $1 * 10^6$
7. $2.23 * 10^{12}$

Study Link 2.9

2. $7 * 10^{-4}$
3. $8 * 10^4$
5. $1 * 10^7$
7. 4,730,000,000
9. 0.0804
11. $1 * 10^{-3}$; 0.001
13. $1 * 10^{-2}, 2 * 10^{-3}, 3 * 10^{-4}$
15. $9.8 * 10^2$
17. $-3 * 10^2$

Use with Lesson 1.12.

Sports Records

Solve.

1. The fastest winning time for the New York Marathon (Juma Ikangaa of Tanzania, 1989) is 2 hours and 8.01 minutes. The second fastest time is 2 hours and 8.12 minutes (John Kagwe of Kenya, 1997).

   How much faster was Ikangaa's time than Kagwe's? _____

2. Driver Buddy Baker (Oldsmobile, 1980) holds the record for the fastest winning speed in the Daytona 500 at 177.602 miles per hour. Bill Elliott (Ford, 1987) has the second fastest speed at 176.263 miles per hour.

   How much faster is Baker's speed than Elliott's? _____

3. The highest scoring World Cup Soccer Final was in 1954. 26 games were played, and 140 goals were scored, for an average of 5.38 goals per game. In 1950, 22 games were played, and 88 goals were scored, for an average of 4 goals per game.

   What is the difference between the 1954 and the 1950 average goals per game?

   _____

4. In the 1908 Olympic Games, Erik Lemming of Sweden won the javelin throw with a distance of 54.825 meters. He won again in 1912 with a distance of 60.64 meters. How much longer was his 1912 throw than his 1908 throw?

   _____

5. $46.09 + 123.047 =$ _____

6. $0.072 + 4.5 =$ _____

7. _____ $= 462.9 + 73.6$

8. _____ $= 0.892 + 0.649$

Multiplying Decimals: Part 1

Multiply.

1.   23   **2.**   56   **3.**   124
          * 87   * 23   * 96

Use your answer for Problem 1 to solve the following problems.

4. 2.3 * 8.7 = _____

5. 23 * 0.87 = _____

6. 2.3 * 87 = _____

Circle the best estimate for each product.

7. 32.05 * 7.89   25   250   2,500

8. 460.32 * 0.093   40   400   4,000

9. 0.98 * 90.07   9   90   900

10. 260.01 * 0.004   1   10   1,000

11. 849.05 * 6.043   50   500   5,000

Place the decimal point in each of the following products.

12. 14.09 * 3.82 = 5 3 8 2 3 8   **13.** 7.8 * 123.6 = 9 6 4 0 8

14. 18.05 * 2.22 = 4 0 0 7 1   **15.** 47.1 * 0.006 = 0 2 8 2 6

Multiplying Decimals: Part 2

Place a decimal point in each problem.

1. 2 4 3 * 7.06 = 171.558

2. 16.4 * 0.7 = 1 1 4 8

3. 8 2 7 * 9.5 = 7.8565

4. 7 5 6 3 * 5.1 = 3,857.13

5. 0.42 * 6.705 = 2 8 1 6 1

Multiply. Show your work on the back of the page.

6. 3.2 * 5.1 = _____

7. 66.7 * 0.8 = _____

8. _____ = 2.28 * 7.9

9. _____ = 49.7 * 0.6

10. _____ = 3.84 * 13

11. 5.9 * 7.6 = _____

Solve each problem. Then write a number model.
(*Hint:* Change the fractions to decimals.)

12. Janine rides her bike at an average speed of 11.8 miles per hour.
At that speed, about how many miles can she ride in $6\frac{1}{2}$ hours? _____

Number Model _____

13. Catherine types at an average rate of 1.25 pages per quarter hour.
If she types for $2\frac{3}{4}$ hours, about how many pages can she type? _____

Number Model _____

14. Find the area in square meters of a
rectangle with length 1.4 m and width 2.9 m. _____

Number Model _____

Decimal Multiplication

Multiply.

1. $4.9 * 0.001 =$ _____

2. _____ $= 7.8 * 0.01$

3. $0.7 * 100 =$ _____

4. _____ $= 0.08 * 10$

5. $30 * 0.1 =$ _____

6. $7 * 0.1 =$ _____

7. $0.15 * 1,000 =$ _____

8. _____ $= 1.9 * 100$

9. For some of the problems below, you need to find the product (and place the decimal point correctly). For others, the multiplication has been done, but the decimal point is missing; you need to place it correctly, using an estimation strategy.

   a. $12.1 * 17 =$ **2 0 5 7**

   b. $4.3 * 0.12 =$ **5 1 6**

   c. $0.50 * 1.6 =$ _____

   d. $0.05 * 101 =$ _____

   e. $3.03 * 9.9 =$ **2 9 9 9 7**

   f. $0.12 * 117 =$ _____

10. The decimal point has been left out of one of the factors in each problem below. Place it correctly.

   a. $2.1 *$ **4 0 3** $= 84.63$

   b. **6 0** $* 3.1 = 18.6$

   c. **9 8 6** $* 1.9 = 187.34$

   d. $4.62 *$ **1 8** $= 8.316$

11. Look at each problem below. Mark how you would find the product—mentally or with paper and pencil. Then find the product.

Problem	Method (circle one)		Product
$117 * 10 = ?$	mental	paper and pencil	
$17 * 4.3 = ?$	mental	paper and pencil	
$14 * 0.5 = ?$	mental	paper and pencil	
$2.071 * 9.8 = ?$	mental	paper and pencil	
$100 * 1.3 = ?$	mental	paper and pencil	

Large Numbers

SRB
4 243

Write the following numbers in standard notation.

1. 3.7 million   _____

2. 0.3 million   _____

3. 44.3 billion   _____

4. 6.5 trillion   _____

5. 0.7 trillion   _____

6. 1,234.5 million   _____

Write the following numbers in number-and-word notation.

7. 4,600,000   _____

8. 7,000,000   _____

9. 83,500,000,000   _____

Tell whether each of the following estimates is reasonable or not reasonable, and explain why you think so. Use 275,000,000 for the population of the United States.

10. Each year, about 1 billion greeting cards are sold in the United States for Valentine's Day.

_____

_____

_____

11. Americans drink about 0.5 billion servings of cola each day.

_____

_____

_____

Source: Astounding Averages

Writing Decimals

1. Build a numeral. Write
   9 in the thousandths place,
   4 in the tenths place,
   8 in the ones place,
   3 in the tens place, and
   6 in the hundredths place.

   Answer:

   ___ ___ . ___ ___ ___

2. Build a numeral. Write
   3 in the tenths place,
   6 in the ten-thousandths place,
   4 in the hundredths place,
   0 in the thousandths place, and
   1 in the ones place.

   Answer:

   ___ . ___ ___ ___ ___

Write the following numbers in words.

3. 0.8 _____

4. 0.95 _____

5. 0.05 _____

6. 0.067 _____

7. 4.0802 _____

Write a decimal place value in each blank space.

8. Bamboo grows at a rate of about 0.00004 or four _____

   of a kilometer per hour.

9. The average speed of a certain brand of catsup from the mouth of the bottle is

   about 0.003 or three _____ of a mile per hour.

10. A three-toed sloth moves at a speed of about 0.068 to 0.098 or sixty-eight

    _____ to ninety-eight _____ of a mile per hour.

Exponential Notation

Write each number in standard notation.

1. 7^2 _____

2. $(0.25)^2$ _____

3. 4^3 _____

4. $(0.41)^3$ _____

5. 10^{-5} _____

6. 4^{-3} _____

Use digits to write each number in exponential notation.

7. three to the ninth power _____

8. eight to the seventh power _____

9. four to the negative third power _____

10. five-tenths to the negative sixth power _____

Write each number as a product of repeated factors.

Example $5^3 = 5 * 5 * 5$

11. $3^4 =$ _____

12. $4^6 =$ _____

13. $10^{-2} =$ _____

14. $10^{-5} =$ _____

Complete the sentences using these words: *exponential notation, exponent, base,* and *factors.*

15. _____ is a shorthand way to write products of repeated

_____. The factor is called the _____.

The number of times it is repeated is indicated by the _____.

Using Scientific Notation

Change the numbers given in scientific notation to standard notation and the numbers given in standard notation to scientific notation.

1. By the year 2000, Tokyo/Yokohama, Japan, was the largest city in the world, with a population of approximately $3 * 10^7$ or _____30,000,000_____ people.

2. The cost of all of the electricity needed to run Disneyland for 1 year is approximately 7,000,000 or _____7×10^6_____ dollars.

3. In one minute, more than $6 * 10^6$ or _____6,000,000_____ chemical reactions may occur in your brain.

4. It takes our galaxy 230,000,000 or _____2.3×10^8_____ years to complete one rotation.

5. The average toll paid by a ship that passes through the Panama Canal is $32,950. The Panama Canal grosses about 1,000,000 or _____1×10^6_____ dollars per day.

6. The average number of thunderstorms in a year is $1.6 * 10^7$ or _____16,000,000_____ thunderstorms.

7. It is estimated that there are about 2,230,000,000,000 or _____2.23×10^{12}_____ grains of sand on the surface of New York's Jones Beach.

8. To buy all of the hogs in Iowa (about 14.8 million hogs at $69 each), you would need approximately 1,000,000,000 or _____1×10^9_____ dollars.

9. A bacterium can travel across a table at a speed of $1.6 * 10^{-4}$ or _____0.00016_____ kilometer per hour.

Sources: Everything Has Its Price; The Sizesaurus; and The Top Ten of Everything

Scientific Notation

Write the following numbers in scientific notation.

1. 0.0036 _____

2. 0.0007 _____

3. 80,000 _____

4. 600 thousand _____

5. 10 million _____

Write the following numbers in standard notation.

6. $5 * 10^4$ _____

7. $4.73 * 10^9$ _____

8. $4.81 * 10^6$ _____

9. $8.04 * 10^{-2}$ _____

10. $6 * 10^{-8}$ _____

Write the next two numbers in each pattern.

11. $1 * 10^{-1}$; 0.1; $1 * 10^{-2}$; 0.01; _____; _____

12. 0.01, 0.002, 0.0003, _____, _____

13. Write the first three numbers of the pattern in Problem 12 in scientific notation.

_____, _____, _____

Solve the following problems. Write each answer in scientific notation.

14. $(4 * 10^3) - 10^2 =$ _____

15. $10^3 - (2 * 10^1) =$ _____

16. $(5 * 10^{-1}) + 0.02 =$ _____

17. $(7 * 10^2) - 10^3 =$ _____

18. $(3 * 10^4) + 5.5 =$ _____

19. Use a calculator to complete the table.

Problem	Calculator Display	Scientific Notation	Standard Notation
$5,000,000^2$			
$90^4 - 300^2$			
$20^3 + 30^2$			
$10^8 * 10^8$			
$5^{20} / 5^{16}$			

Division

3 Ways to Write a Division Problem

$246 \div 12 \to 20$ R6 $12\overline{)246} \to 20$ R6 $246 / 12 \to 20$ R6

Note the arrow, $\to$. We use it because there is a remainder.
$246 / 12 = 20$ R6 would not be a good mathematical sentence.

Use "close" numbers that are easy to divide to estimate the quotients.

Example

346 / 12   Estimate: __*35*__   How I estimated: _*350 / 10 = 35*_

1. 234 / 6   Estimate: _____   How I estimated: _____

2. 659 / 12   Estimate: _____   How I estimated: _____

3. 512 / 9   Estimate: _____   How I estimated: _____

4. 1,270 / 7   Estimate: _____   How I estimated: _____

5. 728 / 34   Estimate: _____   How I estimated: _____

Solve using a division algorithm.

6. 534 / 8 $\to$ _____

7. 976 / 15 $\to$ _____

8. 980 / 20 $\to$ _____

9. 843 / 46 $\to$ _____

10. 6,024 / 38 $\to$ _____

11. 5,586 / 44 $\to$ _____

Division with Decimals

For each problem:

- Estimate the quotient. Use numbers that are close to the numbers given and that are easy to divide. Write your estimate. Write a number sentence to show how you estimated.

- Ignore any decimal points. Divide as if the numbers were whole numbers.

- Use your estimate to insert a decimal point in the final answer.

1. 19.76 ÷ 8

Estimate _____

_____
How I estimated

Answer _____

2. 78.8 / 4

Estimate _____

_____
How I estimated

Answer _____

3. 85.8 / 13

Estimate _____

_____
How I estimated

Answer _____

4. 51.8 / 7

Estimate _____

_____
How I estimated

Answer _____

5. Find 17 ÷ 6. Give the answer as a decimal with two digits after the decimal point.

_____

6. Five people sent a $36 arrangement of flowers to a friend. Divide $36 into 5 equal shares. How much is one share, in dollars and cents?

_____

Family Letter

Unit 3: Variables, Formulas, and Graphs

Variables are symbols—such as *y*, *K*, and *I*—that stand for a specific number or for any number in a range of values. The authors of *Everyday Mathematics* believe that work with variables is too important to be delayed until high-school algebra. The problem "Solve $3x + 40 = 52$" may be difficult for many high-school algebra students because they see it as merely symbol manipulation. Problems like this are posed to *Everyday Mathematics* students as puzzles that can be unraveled by asking, "What number makes the equation true?"

I need to add 12 to 40 to get 52. Three times what number is 12? The answer is 4.

However, algebra consists of more than manipulation of equations containing variables. Variables are also used to generalize patterns, form expressions that show relationships, and express rules and formulas. Unit 3 will focus on these three uses of variables.

Students have worked with "What's My Rule?" tables since the early grades of *Everyday Mathematics*. In this unit, your child will complete tables like the one below, following rules described either in words or with algebraic expressions. Your child will also determine rules or formulas from information given in tables and graphs.

Rule: $y = (4 * x) + -3$

x	y
5	17
2	
0	
	37
	25

In addition, your child will learn how to name cells in a spreadsheet and write formulas to express the relationships among spreadsheet cells. If you use computer spreadsheets at work or at home, you may want to share your experiences with your child. The class will play the game *Spreadsheet Scramble,* in which students practice computation and mental addition of positive and negative numbers. Challenge your child to a round at home!

Please keep this Family Letter for reference as your child works through Unit 3.

Math Tools

Your child will be using **spreadsheets,** a common mathematics tool for the computer. The spreadsheet, similar to the one shown here, gets its name from a ledger sheet for financial records. Such sheets were often large pages, folded or taped, that were *spread* out for examination.

	A	B	C	D
		Class picnic ($$)		
1		budget for class picnic		
2				
3	quantity	food items	unit price	cost
4	6	packages of hamburgers	2.79	16.74
5	5	packages of hamburger buns	1.29	6.45
6	3	bags of potato chips	3.12	9.36
7	3	quarts of macaroni salad	4.50	13.50
8	4	bottles of soft drinks	1.69	6.76
9			subtotal	52.81
10			8% tax	4.23
11			total	57.04

Vocabulary

Important terms in Unit 3:

algebraic expression An expression that contains a variable. For example, if Maria is 2 inches taller than Joe, and if the variable *M* represents Maria's height, then the algebraic expression $M - 2$ represents Joe's height.

cell In a spreadsheet, a box formed where a column and a row intersect. A *column* is a section of cells lined up vertically. A *row* is a section of cells lined up horizontally.

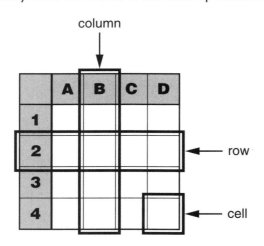

formula A general rule for finding the value of something. A formula is often written using letters, called variables, that stand for the quantities involved. For example, the formula for the area of a rectangle may be written as $A = l * w$, where *A* represents the area of the rectangle, *l* represents its length, and *w* represents its width.

general pattern A model or plan by which elements can be arranged so that what comes next can be predicted.

special case (of a pattern) An instance when values replace the words or variables in a general pattern. For example, $6 + 6 = 12$ is a special case of the pattern $Y + Y = 2Y$.

time graph A graph that is constructed from a story that takes place over time. For example, the time graph below shows the trip Mr. Olds took to drive his son to school. The line shows the increases, decreases, and constant rates of speed that Mr. Olds experienced during the 13-minute trip.

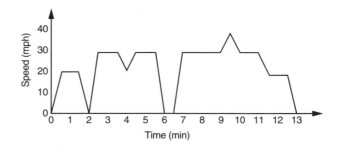

variable A letter or other symbol that represents a number. A variable can represent one specific number, or it can stand for many different numbers.

Do-Anytime Activities

To work with your child on the concepts taught in this unit, try these interesting and rewarding activities:

1 Practice renaming fractions, which is a prerequisite skill for Unit 4. *For example:*

Rename as fractions.

a. $3\frac{1}{2} = \underline{\frac{7}{2}}$

b. $8\frac{1}{3} = \underline{\frac{25}{3}}$

c. $5\frac{3}{4} = \underline{\frac{23}{4}}$

d. $3\frac{1}{3} = \underline{\frac{10}{3}}$

Rename as mixed numbers or whole numbers.

e. $\frac{33}{5} = \underline{6\frac{3}{5}}$

f. $\frac{25}{2} = \underline{12\frac{1}{2}}$

g. $\frac{25}{7} = \underline{3\frac{4}{7}}$

h. $\frac{32}{4} = \underline{8}$

2 If you are planning to paint or carpet a room, consider having your child measure and calculate the area. Have him or her write the formula for area (Area = length * width) and show you the calculations. If the room is an irregular shape, divide it into separate rectangular regions and have your child find the area of each one. If a wall has a cathedral ceiling, imagine a line across the top of the wall to form a triangle. Your child can use the formula Area = $\frac{1}{2}$ * base * height to calculate the area of the triangle.

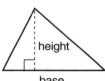

3 If you use a spreadsheet program on a home computer, show your child to learn how to use it. You might help your child set up a spreadsheet to keep track of his or her math scores and to figure out the average.

4 Play *Spreadsheet Scramble* with your child so that he or she can practice operations with positive and negative numbers. The rules are on page 306 of the *Student Reference Book.*

	A	B	C	D	E	F
1						Total
2						
3						
4						
5	Total					

Use with Lesson 2.12.

Family Letter, *continued*

As You Help Your Child with Homework

As your child brings assignments home, you may want to go over the instructions together, clarifying them as necessary. The answers listed below will guide you through some of the Study Links in this unit.

Study Link 3.1

Sample answers are given for Problems 1–5.

1. a. Any value added to zero equals that value.

   b. $36.09 + 0 = 36.09$

2. $406 * 1 = 406$ **3.** $(2 * 24) + 24 = 3 * 24$

4. $(\frac{1}{2} + \frac{1}{2} - 4) * 0 = 0$ **5.** $99 + 0.25 = 0.25 + 99$

6. $n^2 * n^3 = n^5$ **7.** $S * 0.1 = \frac{S}{10}$

8. $x^0 = 1$ **9.** $k^2 = k * k$

Study Link 3.2

5. $a - b = a + (-b)$ **6.** $\frac{c}{d} = \frac{c*3}{d*3}$

7. $\frac{f}{g} = \frac{f \div 2}{g \div 2}$ **8.** $\frac{m}{n} * \frac{1}{2} = \frac{m*1}{n*2}$

Study Link 3.3

1. $P + 45$ **2.** $\frac{4}{5} * S$ **3.** $X - 7$

4. $5 * d$ or $5d$ **5.** $\frac{y}{3}$ or $y \div 3$

6. $3M + 8$, or $(3 * M) + 8$; 44 marbles

7. $\frac{1}{2}S - 4$, or $(\frac{1}{2} * S) - 4$; 6 movies

Study Link 3.4

1. b. $n = m - 0.22$ **2. b.** $r * \frac{1}{2} = t$

3. b. $A = 2 * (B - 1)$

Study Link 3.5

4. Rule: Divide the "in" number by 3.
   Formula: $d = b \div 3$

Study Link 3.6

1. a. $4s$, or $s * 4$

   b. $p = 4s$; $p = s + s + s + s$; $p = (2 * s) + (2 * s)$

2. s^2 **3.**

Perimeter (in.)	Area (in.²)
4	1
8	4
12	9
16	16
20	25

5. 10 in.   **6.** 17 in.   **8.** $2\frac{1}{4}$ in.²   **9.** $10\frac{1}{2}$ in.²

Study Link 3.7

1. January **2.** $115.95 **3.** A5   **4.** C3

6. E3 = B3 + C3 + D3 **7.** E5 = B5 + C5 + D5

8. $128.75

Study Link 3.8

1. 8   **2.** 2   **3.** -15 **4.** -5

5. -13 **6.** -12 **7.** $b = -7$ **8.** $a = 4$

9. $m = -7$ **10.** $k = 4$

11. a. Sample answer: Add negative 6 to every value in the x column.

11. b. $x + (-6) = y$

Study Link 3.9

1. Sample answer: People are getting on the Ferris wheel.

2. 125 sec **3.** 170 sec **4.** 4 times **5.** 40 sec

Study Link 3.10

1.

Jenna's Profit	Thomas's Profit
$3.00	$6.00
$6.00	$8.00
$9.00	$10.00
$12.00	$12.00
$15.00	$14.00
$18.00	$16.00

3. Sample answer: It depends on the length of the job. Jenna has a better system for longer jobs because after 4 hours of babysitting, she is earning more than Thomas. But Thomas will earn more on short jobs, such as when the parent is just going to the grocery store and will only be gone for about $1\frac{1}{2}$ hours.

Variables in Number Patterns

1. Here are three special cases representing a general pattern.

$$17 + 0 = 17 \qquad\qquad -43 + 0 = -43 \qquad\qquad \frac{7}{8} + 0 = \frac{7}{8}$$

SRB
101

a. Describe the general pattern in words.

_____

b. Give two other special cases for the pattern.

_____   _____

For each general pattern, give two special cases.

2. $L * 1 = L$

_____   _____

3. $(2 * m) + m = 3 * m$

_____   _____

4. $(R + R - 4) * 0 = 0$

_____   _____

5. $s + 0.25 = 0.25 + s$

_____   _____

For each set of special cases, write a general pattern.

6. $3^2 * 3^3 = 3^5$

    $5^2 * 5^3 = 5^5$

    $13^2 * 13^3 = 13^5$

    _____

7. $7 * 0.1 = \frac{7}{10}$

    $3 * 0.1 = \frac{3}{10}$

    $4 * 0.1 = \frac{4}{10}$

    _____

8. $2^0 = 1$

    $146^0 = 1$

    $\left(\frac{1}{2}\right)^0 = 1$

    _____

9. $3^2 = 3 * 3$

    $6^2 = 6 * 6$

    $0.7^2 = 0.7 * 0.7$

    _____

General Patterns with Two Variables

For each general pattern, write two special cases.

1. $4 * (a + b) = (4 * a) + (4 * b)$ _____

_____

2. $(6 * b) * c = 6 * (b * c)$ _____

_____

3. $a \div \dfrac{b}{2} = (2 * a) \div b$ _____

(b is not 0.) _____

4. $\dfrac{x}{y} = x * \dfrac{1}{y}$ _____

(y is not 0.) _____

For each set of special cases, write a number sentence with two variables to describe the general pattern.

5. $7 - 5 = 7 + (-5)$

$12 - 8 = 12 + (-8)$

$9 - 1 = 9 + (-1)$

General pattern:

_____

6. $\dfrac{4}{6} = \dfrac{4 * 3}{6 * 3}$

$\dfrac{1}{2} = \dfrac{1 * 3}{2 * 3}$

$\dfrac{2}{5} = \dfrac{2 * 3}{5 * 3}$

General pattern:

_____

7. $\dfrac{6}{10} = \dfrac{6 \div 2}{10 \div 2}$

$\dfrac{4}{12} = \dfrac{4 \div 2}{12 \div 2}$

$\dfrac{2}{4} = \dfrac{2 \div 2}{4 \div 2}$

General pattern:

_____

8. $\dfrac{1}{5} * \dfrac{1}{2} = \dfrac{1 * 1}{5 * 2}$

$\dfrac{2}{3} * \dfrac{1}{2} = \dfrac{2 * 1}{3 * 2}$

$\dfrac{3}{4} * \dfrac{1}{2} = \dfrac{3 * 1}{4 * 2}$

General pattern:

_____

Algebraic Expressions

Write an algebraic expression for each situation. Use the suggested variable.

SRB
222

1. Frank weighs 45 pounds more than Elaine.
   If Elaine weighs *P* pounds, how much does
   Frank weigh?   _p + 45_   pounds

2. Bill swam for $\frac{4}{5}$ the length of time that Ken swam.
   If Ken swam for *S* minutes, for how long did
   Bill swim? $\frac{4}{5} \cdot s$ minutes

3. Jennifer has *X* CDs in her collection. If Caitlin
   has 7 fewer CDs than Jennifer, how many CDs
   does Caitlin have?   _X − 7_   CDs

4. Steven has *d* dollars. Tara has 5 times as
   much money as Steven. How much money
   does Tara have?   _d · 5_   dollars

5. Mary Jo has been a lifeguard for *y* years. That
   is 3 times as many years as Scott has been a
   lifeguard. How long has Scott been a lifeguard?   _y ÷ 3_   years

First translate each situation from words into an algebraic expression.
Then solve the problem that follows.

6. Monica has 8 more marbles than 3 times the
   number of marbles Greg has. If Greg has *M*
   marbles, how many does Monica have?   _3 · m + 8_   marbles

   If Greg has 12 marbles, how many does
   Monica have?   _3 · 12 + 8 = 44_   marbles

7. Hannah has seen 4 fewer than $\frac{1}{2}$ the number
   of movies that her sister has seen. If her sister
   has seen *S* movies, how many has Hannah seen? $\frac{1}{2} \cdot s - 4$ movies

   If her sister has seen 20 movies, how many
   has Hannah seen? $\frac{1}{2} \cdot 20 - 4 = 6$ movies

"What's My Rule?" 1

1. a. State in words the rule for the "What's My Rule?" table at the right.

SRB
227 235

_____

_____

_____

m	n
4.56	4.34
10	9.78
0.01	−0.21
$\frac{24}{100}$	0.02
7.80	7.58

b. Circle the formula that describes the rule.

$n = m - 0.22$ $m + n = 0.22$ $m = n - 0.22$

2. a. State in words the rule for the "What's My Rule?" table at the right.

_____

_____

_____

r	t
20	10
15	7.5
1	0.5
$\frac{3}{2}$	$\frac{3}{4}$
3.4	1.7

b. Circle the formula that describes the rule.

$r - \frac{1}{4} = t$ $t + \frac{1}{6} = r$ $r * \frac{1}{2} = t$

3. a. State in words the rule for the "What's My Rule?" table at the right.

_____

_____

_____

A	B
12	7
18	10
0	1
28	15
58	30

b. Circle the formula that describes the rule.

$A - 13 = B$ $A = (2 * B) - 1$ $A = 2 * (B - 1)$

"What's My Rule?" 2

Complete each table for the given rule or formula.

1. *Rule:* Subtract the "in" number from $11\frac{1}{2}$

in	out
n	$11\frac{1}{2} - n$
1	
2	
$8\frac{1}{2}$	
	5
18	
	$-\frac{1}{2}$

2. *Formula:* $r = 4 * s$

in	out
s	$4 * s$
7	28
12	
	24
0.3	
	1
$\frac{1}{2}$	

3. *Rule:* Triple the "in" number and add -6

in	out
x	$(3 * x) + (-6)$
1	-3
2	
3	3
	15
8	
	-6

4. For the table below, write the rule both in words and as a formula.

Rule: _____

_____

Formula: _____

5. Make up your own.

Rule: _____

_____

Formula: _____

in	out
b	d
1.5	0.5
$6\frac{3}{4}$	$2\frac{1}{4}$
9.75	3.25
24	8
-12	-4
81	27

in	out
q	y

Area and Perimeter

1. **a.** Write a formula to find the perimeter (*p*) of a square.
   Use *s* to represent the length of a side.

   s

   $p =$ _____

   b. Write another formula to find the perimeter of a square.

   _____

2. Write a formula to find the area (*A*) of a square. Use *s* to represent the
   length of a side.

   $A =$ _____

3. Use the perimeter and area formulas for squares to complete the table.

Length of side (in.)	Perimeter (in.)	Area (in.²)
1		
2		
3		
4		
5		

4. Graph the perimeter data on the grid at the right.

Use the graph you made in Problem 4 to answer the following questions.

5. If the length of the side of a square is $2\frac{1}{2}$ inches, what is the perimeter of the square?

_____
(unit)

6. If the length of the side of a square is $4\frac{1}{4}$ inches, what is the perimeter of the square?

_____
(unit)

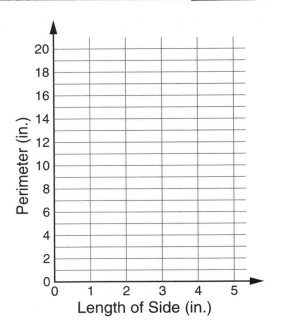

7. Graph the area data on the grid at the right.

Use the graph you made in Problem 7 to answer the following questions.

8. If the length of the side of a square is $1\frac{1}{2}$ inches, what is the approximate area of the square?

About _____
(unit)

9. If the length of the side of a square is $3\frac{1}{4}$ inches, what is the approximate area of the square?

About _____
(unit)

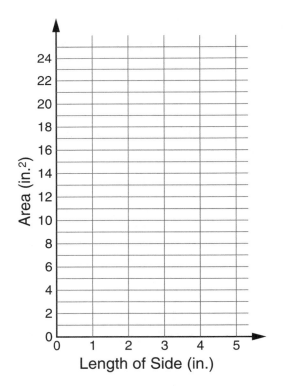

Spreadsheet Practice

Ms. Villanova keeps a spreadsheet of her monthly expenses. Use her spreadsheet to answer the questions below.

	A	B	C	D	E
1		January	February	March	Total
2	Groceries	$125.25	$98.00	$138.80	$362.05
3	Phone Bill	$34.90	$58.50	$25.35	
4	Car Expenses	$25.00	$115.95	$12.00	
5	Rent	$750.00	$750.00	$750.00	

1. What is shown in Cell B1? _____

2. What is shown in Cell C4? _____

3. Which cell contains the word *Rent?* _____

4. Which cell contains the amount $58.50? _____

5. Ms. Villanova used Column E to show the total for each row. Find the missing totals and enter them on the spreadsheet.

6. Write a formula for calculating E3 that uses cell names. _____

7. Write a formula for calculating E5 that uses cell names. _____

8. Ms. Villanova found that she made a mistake in recording her March phone bill. Instead of $25.35, she should have entered $35.35. After she corrects her spreadsheet, what will the new total be in Cell E3?

_____

Add Positive and Negative Numbers

Add.

1. $13 + (-5) =$ _____

2. $(-10) + 12 =$ _____

3. _____ $= (-7) + (-8)$

4. _____ $= (-15) + 10$

5. $(-4) + (-9) =$ _____

6. _____ $= 7 + (-19)$

Solve.

7. $b + 10 = 3$ _____

8. $-5 + a = -1$ _____

9. $m + (-7) = -14$ _____

10. $k + 9 = 13$ _____

11. Complete the "What's My Rule?" table.

x	y
10	4
18	12
5	−1
0	
2	
	−15
	7

a. State, in words, the rule for the table.

_____

_____

b. Circle the formula that describes the rule.

$x + 6 = y$ $x * (-6) = y$

$x + (-6) = y$ $x / 6 = y$

Ferris Wheel Time Graph

The time graph below shows the height of Rose's head from the ground as she rides a Ferris wheel. Use the graph to answer the following questions.

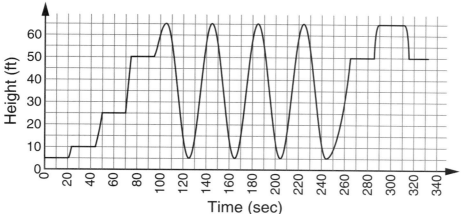

1. Explain what is happening from 0 to 95 seconds. _____

_____

2. How long is Rose on the Ferris wheel before she
is back to the position from which she started?   About _____

                                                                            (unit)

3. Once the Ferris wheel has been completely loaded,
about how long does the ride last before unloading begins? _____

                                                                            (unit)

4. Once the Ferris wheel has been loaded, how many
times does the wheel go around before unloading begins? _____

                                                                            (unit)

5. Once the ride is in full swing, approximately how
long does one complete revolution of the wheel take?   _____

                                                                            (unit)

Challenge

6. Rose takes another
ride. After 130
seconds, the Ferris
wheel comes to a
complete stop because
of an electrical failure.
It starts moving again
2 minutes later.
Complete the graph to
show this event.

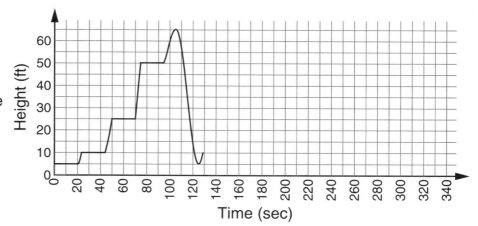

Comparing Babysitting Profits

Jenna and Thomas like to babysit. Jenna charges $3 per hour. Thomas charges $6.00 for the first hour and $2 for each additional hour.

1. Complete the table to show how much each babysitter will have made after 1 hour, 2 hours, 3 hours, and so on.

Time (hours)	Jenna's Profit	Thomas's Profit
1		
2		
3		
4		
5		
6		

2. Use the grid to graph the babysitters' profits. Label the lines "Jenna" and "Thomas."

3. Did Jenna or Thomas think of a better way to charge customers? Explain your answer.

_____

_____

_____

_____

_____

_____

_____

_____

_____

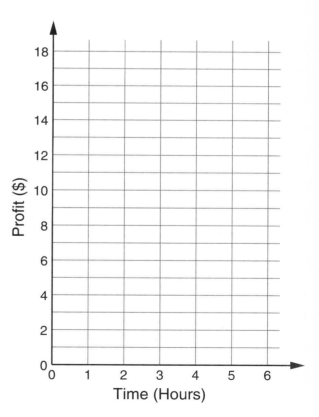

Family Letter

Unit 4: Rational Number Uses and Operations

One reason for studying mathematics is that numbers in all their forms are an important part of our everyday lives. We use decimals when dealing with measures and money, and we use fractions and percents to describe parts of things.

Students using *Everyday Mathematics* began working with fractions in the primary grades. In *Fifth Grade Everyday Mathematics*, your child worked with equivalent fractions, operations with fractions, and conversions between fractions, decimals, and percents.

In Unit 4, your child will revisit these concepts and expand on them. Most of the fractions we will work with—halves, thirds, fourths, sixths, eighths, tenths, and twelfths—will be fractions that occur in everyday situations: interpreting scale drawings, following a recipe, measuring distance and area, expressing time in fractions of hours, and so on.

Students will be exploring methods for solving addition and subtraction problems with fractions and mixed numbers. They will look at estimation strategies, mental computation methods, pencil-and-paper algorithms, and calculator procedures.

Students will also work with multiplication of fractions and mixed numbers. Generally, verbal cues are a poor guide to which operation $(+, -, *, /)$ to use when solving a problem. For example, "more" does not necessarily signal "add." But "many of" and "part of" do seem to be closely tied to multiplication. Your child is more likely to succeed when responding to $\frac{1}{2} * 12$ as "one-half of 12," rather than as "one-half times 12"; or to $\frac{1}{2} * \frac{1}{2}$ as "one-half of one-half," rather than as "one-half times one-half."

Finally, students will use percents to make circle graphs to display the results of surveys and to learn about sales and discounts.

Jambalaya

$\frac{3}{4}$ cup rice

4 ounces each of chicken and sausage

4 cups peppers

$1\frac{2}{3}$ cups chopped onions

$1\frac{1}{2}$ tablespoons chopped thyme

$\frac{1}{8}$ teaspoon salt

Please keep this Family Letter for reference as your child works through Unit 4.

Math Tools

The **Percent Circle,** on the Geometry Template, is used to find the percent represented by each part of a circle graph and to make circle graphs. The Percent Circle is similar to a full-circle protractor with the circumference marked in percents rather than degrees. This tool allows students to interpret and make circle graphs before they are ready for the complex calculations needed to make circle graphs with a protractor.

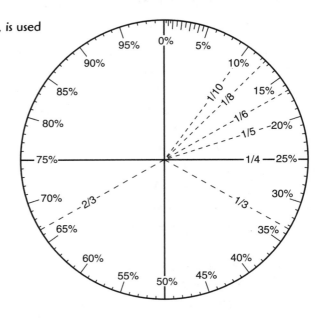

Vocabulary

Important terms in Unit 4:

common factor A number that is a factor of two or more numbers. For example, 4 is a common factor of 8 and 12 because $8 = 4 * 2$ and $12 = 4 * 3$.

common multiple A number that is a multiple of two or more numbers. For example, 24 is a common multiple of 8 and 12 because $24 = 8 * 3$ and $24 = 12 * 2$.

equivalent fractions Fractions that have different denominators but name the same amount. For example, $\frac{1}{2}$ and $\frac{4}{8}$ are equivalent fractions.

greatest common factor (GCF) The largest common factor of two or more numbers. For example, the common factors of 24 and 36 are 1, 2, 3, 4, 6, and 12; the greatest common factor of 24 and 36 is 12.

improper fraction A fraction whose numerator is greater than or equal to its denominator. For example, $\frac{4}{3}, \frac{5}{2}, \frac{4}{4}$, and $\frac{24}{12}$ are improper fractions. In *Everyday Mathematics,* improper fractions are sometimes called "top-heavy" fractions.

least common denominator (LCD) The smallest common multiple of the denominators of every fraction in a given collection. For example, the least common denominator of $\frac{1}{2}, \frac{4}{5}$, and $\frac{3}{8}$ is 40.

quick common denominator (QCD) The product of the denominators of two or more fractions. For example the QCD of $\frac{1}{4}$ and $\frac{3}{6}$ is $4 * 6$, or 24. As the name suggests, this is a quick way to get a common denominator for a collection of fractions, but it does not necessarily give the *least common denominator.*

simplest form A fraction less than 1 is in simplest form if there is no number other than 1 that divides its numerator and denominator evenly. A mixed number is in simplest form if its fractional part is in simplest form.

Use with Lesson 3.11.

Do-Anytime Activities

To work with your child on the concepts taught in this unit, try these interesting and rewarding activities:

1 Consider allowing your sixth grader to accompany you on shopping trips when you know there is a sale. Have your child bring a calculator to figure out the sale price of items. Have your child show you the sale price of the item and the amount of the discount. If your child enjoys this activity, you might extend it by letting him or her figure out the tax of the item as well. Simply multiply 0.0825, for $8\frac{1}{4}$% tax, (or whatever the sales tax is in your area, 0.07 for 7%, and so on) by the cost of the item. ($19.95 $*$ 0.0825 = 1.645875; or $1.65 in tax)

2 On grocery shopping trips, point out to your child the decimals printed on the item labels on the shelves. These often show unit prices per ounce, or per gram, reported to 3 or 4 decimal places. Have your child round the numbers to the nearest hundredth (the second place to the right of the decimal point).

3 Consider asking your child to double or triple recipes for you, whenever you are planning to do that. Watch your child to make sure he or she does the math for every ingredient. Or, your child can halve a recipe if your cooking plans call for smaller amounts.

4 If you have hobbies such as carpentry or sewing, consider having your child measure, cut, or add and subtract measures for you. Expect him or her to be able to measure to the nearest eighth of an inch, and to be able to add and subtract such measures.

Building Skills through Games

In Unit 4, your child will work on his or her understanding of rational numbers by playing the following games. For detailed instructions, see the *Student Reference Book.*

Buzz *See Student Reference Book, page 281*
No materials are required for this game. 5–10 players sit in a circle to play *Buzz* The goal of the game is to strengthen the skill of recognizing multiples of a given number.

Frac-Tac-Toe *See Student Reference Book, pages 290–292*
Two players need a deck of number cards with 4 each of the numbers 0–10; a gameboard, a 5-by-5 grid that resembles a bingo card; a *Frac-Tac-Toe* Number-Card Board; markers or counters in two different colors; and a calculator. The three versions, *2-4-5-10 Frac-Tac-Toe, 2-4-5-8-10 Frac-Tac-Toe,* and *2-4-8 Frac-Tac-Toe,* help students practice conversions between fractions, decimals, and percents.

Use with Lesson 3.11.

As You Help Your Child with Homework

As your child brings assignments home, you may want to go over the instructions together, clarifying them as necessary. The answers listed below will guide you through some of this unit's Study Links.

Study Link 4.1

17. $\frac{1}{2}$ **18.** $\frac{2}{3}$ **19.** $\frac{1}{5}$

20. $\frac{2}{5}$ **21.** $\frac{3}{8}$ **22.** $\frac{2}{7}$

23. $x = 3$ **24.** $y = 12$

25. $k = 6$ **26.** $m = 30$

Study Link 4.2

1. $>$ **2.** $>$ **3.** $<$

4. $<$ **5.** $>$ **6.** $<$

7. $\frac{1}{3}, \frac{2}{5}, \frac{12}{25}$

8. $0, \frac{1}{12}, \frac{1}{5}, \frac{1}{3}, \frac{2}{5}, \frac{7}{14}, \frac{6}{10}, \frac{15}{16}, \frac{49}{50}, 1$

Study Link 4.3

1. $\frac{1}{2}$ **2.** $1\frac{1}{16}$ **3.** $2\frac{13}{20}$ **4.** $\frac{2}{3}$

5. $\frac{11}{12}$ **6.** $1\frac{1}{6}$ **7.** $1\frac{8}{45}$ **8.** 2

9. $\frac{3}{8}$ **10.** $1\frac{4}{15}$ **11.** $\frac{1}{3}$ **12.** $\frac{1}{2}$

13. $1\frac{3}{4}$ **14.** $\frac{1}{10}$ **15.** $\frac{1}{2}$ **16.** 0

Study Link 4.4

1. **a.** Sample answer: Those students may have added just the numerators.

    b. Sample answer: Both fractions are close to 1, so their sum should be close to 2.

2. $1\frac{1}{4}$ inches

3. Sample answer: He can use three $\frac{1}{2}$-cup measures and one $\frac{1}{4}$- cup measure.

4. $4\frac{1}{2}$ **5.** $1\frac{3}{4}$ **6.** 4

7. $2\frac{1}{3}$ **8.** $1\frac{7}{4}, \frac{11}{4}$ **9.** $2\frac{4}{3}, \frac{10}{3}, 2\frac{8}{6}$

Study Link 4.5

1. **a.** $8\frac{1}{2}$ inches   **b.** $1\frac{1}{2}$ inches; $\frac{1}{4}$ inch

2. **a.** $2\frac{1}{2}$ bushels   **b.** 30 quarts

3. 4 **4.** $\frac{2}{3}$ **5.** $5\frac{1}{6}$

6. $\frac{5}{9}$ **7.** $1\frac{5}{8}$ **8.** 6

9. $(1\frac{1}{2} + 2\frac{1}{2}) + (4\frac{2}{3} + 5\frac{1}{3}) = 4 + 10 = 14$

Study Link 4.6

1. $\frac{6}{20}$ **2.** $\frac{15}{63}$ **3.** $\frac{15}{8}$ **4.** $\frac{11}{48}$

5. $\frac{35}{48}$ **6.** $\frac{21}{100}$ **7.** $\frac{14}{45}$ **8.** $\frac{32}{7}$

9. $\frac{1}{5}$ of the points   **10.** $2\frac{1}{4}$ cups

11. $\frac{7}{12}$ of the sixth graders

12. **a.** $\frac{1}{2}$ of the girls

    b. 6 girls

Study Link 4.7

1. $\frac{9}{5}$ **2.** $\frac{18}{6}$ **3.** $\frac{17}{3}$ **4.** $\frac{7}{2}$

5. 3 **6.** $4\frac{1}{8}$ **7.** $2\frac{1}{2}$ **8.** $6\frac{2}{3}$

9. 3 **10.** $4\frac{1}{5}$ **11.** $2\frac{1}{12}$ **12.** $5\frac{4}{9}$

13. $7\frac{31}{32}$ **14.** 20

Study Link 4.8

1. $\frac{8}{10}$, 80%   **2.** $\frac{75}{100}$, 75% **3.** $\frac{30}{100}, \frac{3}{10}$ **4.** 0.5

5. 0.75 **6.** 0.25 **7.** 1.8 **8.** $\frac{2}{5}$

9. $\frac{1}{10}$ **10.** $\frac{17}{25}$ **11.** $\frac{1}{4}$ **12.** 50%

13. 25%   **14.** 60%   **15.** 95%   **16.** $\frac{50}{100}, \frac{1}{2}$

17. $\frac{40}{100}, \frac{2}{5}$ **18.** $\frac{100}{100}, 1$ **19.** $\frac{180}{100}, 1\frac{4}{5}$

Study Link 4.9

1. 65%   **2.** 33.4%   **3.** 2%

4. 40%   **5.** 270%   **6.** 309%

7. 0.27   **8.** 0.539   **9.** 0.08

10. 0.6   **11.** 1.8   **12.** 1.15

13. 0.88, 88%   **14.** 0.43, 43%   **15.** 0.42, 42%

Equivalent Fractions

Find an equivalent fraction by multiplying.

1. $\frac{4}{5}$ _____

2. $\frac{7}{10}$ _____

3. $\frac{5}{4}$ _____

4. $\frac{1}{4}$ _____

5. $\frac{2}{3}$ _____

6. $\frac{2}{2}$ _____

Find an equivalent fraction by dividing.

7. $\frac{9}{12}$ _____

8. $\frac{20}{100}$ _____

9. $\frac{4}{16}$ _____

10. $\frac{30}{12}$ _____

11. $\frac{10}{50}$ _____

12. $\frac{16}{24}$ _____

Write three equivalent fractions for each number.

13. $\frac{1}{3}$ _____

14. $\frac{75}{100}$ _____

15. 6 _____

16. $\frac{12}{5}$ _____

Write each fraction in simplest form.

17. $\frac{8}{16}$ _____

18. $\frac{6}{9}$ _____

19. $\frac{3}{15}$ _____

20. $\frac{10}{25}$ _____

21. $\frac{6}{16}$ _____

22. $\frac{14}{49}$ _____

Find the missing numbers.

23. $\frac{1}{5} = \frac{x}{15}$

$x =$ _____

24. $\frac{2}{3} = \frac{y}{18}$

$y =$ _____

25. $\frac{3}{4} = \frac{k}{8}$

$k =$ _____

26. $\frac{15}{25} = \frac{m}{50}$

$m =$ _____

Comparing and Ordering Fractions

Write <, >, or = to make a true number sentence. Put a star next to each problem that you were able to solve mentally. Be prepared to explain how you solved it. For each problem that you did not solve mentally, show how you got the answer.

1. $\frac{4}{5}$ _____ $\frac{2}{5}$

2. $\frac{3}{8}$ _____ $\frac{1}{3}$

3. $\frac{3}{4}$ _____ $\frac{17}{20}$

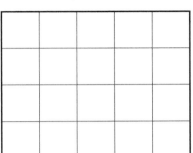
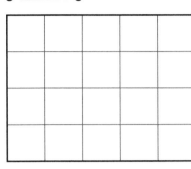
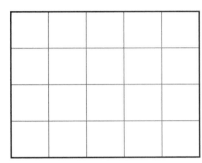

4. $\frac{19}{20}$ _____ $\frac{99}{100}$

5. $\frac{4}{7}$ _____ $\frac{4}{10}$

6. $\frac{2}{3}$ _____ $\frac{7}{9}$

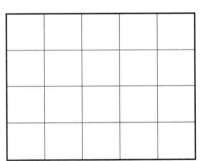
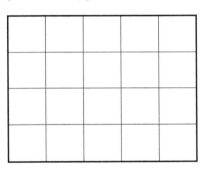
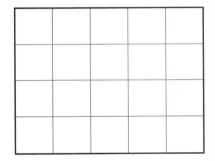

7. Circle each fraction that is less than $\frac{1}{2}$.

$\frac{3}{6}$ $\frac{6}{10}$ $\frac{1}{3}$ $\frac{2}{5}$ $\frac{6}{11}$ $\frac{12}{25}$

8. Write the fractions in order from smallest to largest.

$\frac{1}{3}$ $\frac{15}{16}$ $\frac{7}{14}$ $\frac{1}{5}$ $\frac{2}{5}$ $\frac{49}{50}$ $\frac{6}{10}$ $\frac{1}{12}$

0 _____ _____ _____ _____ _____ _____ _____ _____ 1

Adding and Subtracting Fractions

Add or subtract. Write each answer in simplest form. If possible, rename answers as mixed numbers or whole numbers.

1. $\frac{1}{3} + \frac{1}{6} =$ _____

2. $\frac{3}{4} + \frac{5}{16} =$ _____

3. $\frac{9}{4} + \frac{2}{5} =$ _____

4. $\frac{2}{9} + \frac{4}{9} =$ _____

5. $\frac{1}{6} + \frac{3}{4} =$ _____

6. $\frac{5}{12} + \frac{3}{4} =$ _____

7. $\frac{7}{9} + \frac{2}{5} =$ _____

8. $\frac{5}{4} + \frac{3}{4} =$ _____

9. $\frac{7}{8} - \frac{2}{4} =$ _____

10. $\frac{5}{3} - \frac{2}{5} =$ _____

11. $\frac{11}{12} - \frac{7}{12} =$ _____

12. $\frac{4}{5} - \frac{3}{10} =$ _____

13. $\frac{15}{8} - \frac{3}{24} =$ _____

14. $\frac{3}{5} - \frac{1}{2} =$ _____

15. $\frac{2}{3} - \frac{1}{6} =$ _____

16. $\frac{5}{6} - \frac{10}{12} =$ _____

+, − Fractions and Mixed Numbers

1. In a national test, eighth grade students were given the problem at the right. Also shown are the five possible answers they were given and the percent of students who chose each answer.

   a. What mistake do you think was made by the students who chose C?

   _____

   _____

   b. Answer B is the best estimate. Explain why.

   _____

   _____

   _____

   Estimate the answer to $\frac{12}{13} + \frac{7}{8}$.
   You will not have enough time to solve the problem using paper and pencil.

Possible Answers		Percent Who Chose This Answer
A.	1	7%
B.	2	24%
C.	19	28%
D.	21	27%
E.	I don't know	14%

2. A board is $6\frac{3}{8}$ inches long. Verna wants to cut off enough so that it will be $5\frac{1}{8}$ inches long. How much should she cut off? _____
   (unit)

3. Tim is making papier-mâché. The recipe calls for $1\frac{3}{4}$ cups of paste. Using only $\frac{1}{2}$-cup, $\frac{1}{4}$-cup, and $\frac{1}{3}$-cup measures, how can he measure the correct amount?

   _____

   _____

Add or subtract. Write your answers as mixed numbers in simplest form. Show your work on the back of the page. Use number sense to check whether each answer is reasonable.

4. $3\frac{1}{4} + 1\frac{1}{4} =$ _____

5. $4 - 2\frac{1}{4} =$ _____

6. $6\frac{1}{4} - 2\frac{1}{4} =$ _____

7. $1\frac{2}{3} + \frac{2}{3} =$ _____

8. Circle the numbers that are equivalent to $2\frac{3}{4}$.

   $1\frac{7}{4}$ $\qquad$ $\frac{6}{4}$ $\qquad$ $\frac{3}{7}$ $\qquad$ $\frac{11}{4}$

9. Circle the numbers that are equivalent to $3\frac{1}{3}$.

   $2\frac{4}{3}$ $\qquad$ $\frac{4}{3}$ $\qquad$ $\frac{10}{3}$ $\qquad$ $2\frac{8}{6}$

Mixed-Number Practice

1. Answer the following questions about the rectangle at the right. Include measure units in your answers.

   $2\frac{3}{4}$ in.

   a. What is the perimeter? _____

   $1\frac{1}{2}$ in.

   b. If you were to trim this rectangle so that it was a square measuring $1\frac{1}{4}$ inches on a side, how much would you cut off

   from the base? _____   from the height? _____

2. Jonathan bought a peck of Jonathan apples, a peck of Golden Delicious apples, a half-bushel of Red Delicious apples, and $1\frac{1}{2}$ bushels of McIntosh apples.

   1 peck = $\frac{1}{4}$ bushel

   a. How many bushels of apples did he buy in all? _____

   b. Jonathan estimates that he can make about 12 quarts of applesauce per bushel of apples. About how many quarts of applesauce can he make from the apples he bought?   _____

Add or subtract. Show your work on the back of the page.

3. $2\frac{1}{3} + 1\frac{2}{3} =$ _____

4. $6\frac{1}{3} - 5\frac{2}{3} =$ _____

5. $4\frac{1}{2} + \frac{2}{3} =$ _____

6. $6 - 5\frac{4}{9} =$ _____

7. $4\frac{3}{8} - 2\frac{3}{4} =$ _____

8. $3\frac{1}{4} + 2\frac{3}{4} =$ _____

Challenge

9. There is an easy way to add the following four fractions without finding a common denominator. Rewrite the problem to show the shortcut.

   $1\frac{1}{2} + 4\frac{2}{3} + 2\frac{1}{2} + 5\frac{1}{3} = ?$

_____

Fraction Multiplication

Use the fraction multiplication algorithm below to solve the following problems.

> **Fraction Multiplication Algorithm**
>
> $$\frac{a}{b} * \frac{c}{d} = \frac{a * c}{b * d}$$

1. $\frac{3}{5} * \frac{2}{4} =$ _____

2. $\frac{3}{7} * \frac{5}{9} =$ _____

3. $5 * \frac{3}{8} =$ _____

4. _____ $= \frac{11}{12} * \frac{1}{4}$

5. $\frac{5}{6} * \frac{7}{8} =$ _____

6. $\frac{3}{10} * \frac{7}{10} =$ _____

7. _____ $= \frac{2}{5} * \frac{7}{9}$

8. $\frac{4}{7} * 8 =$ _____

9. South High beat North High in basketball, scoring $\frac{4}{5}$ of the total points. Rachel scored $\frac{1}{4}$ of South High's points. What fraction of the total points did Rachel score?

(*Hint:* Remember that *of* indicates multiplication.) _____

10. Josh was making raisin muffins for a party. He needed to triple the recipe, which called for $\frac{3}{4}$ cup of raisins. How many cups of raisins did he need? _____

11. At the Ashley Long Middle School, $\frac{7}{8}$ of the sixth graders live within one mile of the school. About $\frac{2}{3}$ of those sixth graders walk to school. None who live a mile or more away walk to school. About what fraction of the sixth graders walk to school? _____

12. a. For Calista's 12th birthday party, her mom will order pizza. $\frac{3}{4}$ of the girls like vegetables on their pizza. However, $\frac{1}{3}$ of those girls don't like green peppers. What fraction of all the girls will eat a green pepper and onion pizza? _____

b. If 12 girls are at the party (including Calista) how many girls will *not* eat a green pepper and onion pizza? _____

Multiplying Mixed Numbers

Rename each mixed number as a fraction.

1. $1\frac{4}{5}$ _____

2. $2\frac{6}{6}$ _____

3. $5\frac{2}{3}$ _____

4. $3\frac{1}{2}$ _____

Rename each fraction as a mixed number or whole number.

5. $\frac{12}{4}$ _____

6. $\frac{33}{8}$ _____

7. $\frac{15}{6}$ _____

8. $\frac{20}{3}$ _____

Multiply. Write each answer in simplest form. If possible, write answers as mixed numbers or whole numbers.

9. $5 * \frac{3}{5} =$ _____

10. $2\frac{1}{3} * 1\frac{4}{5} =$ _____

11. $\frac{5}{6} * 2\frac{1}{2} =$ _____

12. $1\frac{1}{6} * 4\frac{2}{3} =$ _____

13. $3\frac{3}{4} * 2\frac{1}{8} =$ _____

14. $7\frac{1}{2} * 2\frac{2}{3} =$ _____

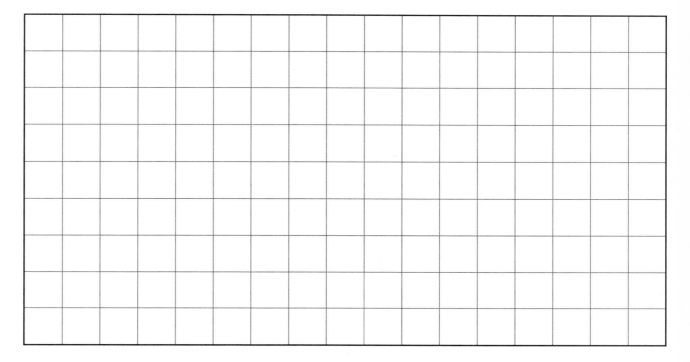

Fractions, Decimals, and Percents

Study Link 4.8

Fill in the missing numbers below. Then shade each large square to represent all three of the equivalent numbers below it. Each large square is worth 1.

1.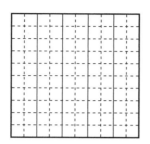

$$\frac{4}{5} = \frac{\boxed{}}{10} = \underline{}\%$$

2.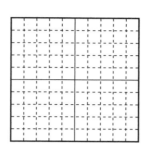

$$\frac{6}{8} = \frac{\boxed{}}{100} = \underline{}\%$$

3.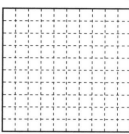

$$30\% = \frac{\boxed{}}{100} = \frac{\boxed{}}{10}$$

Rename the fractions as decimals.

4. $\frac{7}{14} = \underline{}$ **5.** $\frac{6}{8} = \underline{}$ **6.** $\frac{5}{20} = \underline{}$ **7.** $1\frac{4}{5} = \underline{}$

Rename the decimals as fractions in simplest form.

8. $0.4 = \underline{}$ **9.** $0.10 = \underline{}$ **10.** $0.68 = \underline{}$ **11.** $0.25 = \underline{}$

Rename the fractions as percents.

12. $\frac{25}{50} = \underline{}$ **13.** $\frac{6}{24} = \underline{}$ **14.** $\frac{18}{30} = \underline{}$ **15.** $\frac{19}{20} = \underline{}$

Rename the percents as fractions in simplest form.

16. $50\% = \frac{\boxed{}}{100} = \underline{}$ **17.** $40\% = \frac{\boxed{}}{100} = \underline{}$

18. $100\% = \frac{\boxed{}}{100} = \underline{}$ **19.** $180\% = \frac{\boxed{}}{100} = \underline{}$

Experiment

Often, people don't realize that fractions, decimals, and percents are numbers. To them, numbers are whole numbers like 1, 5, or 100. Try the following experiment: Ask several adults to name four numbers between 1 and 10. Then ask several children. Keep a record of all responses on the back of this paper. How many named fractions, decimals, or percents? Now ask the same people to name four numbers between 1 and 3. Report your findings tomorrow.

Decimals, Percents, and Fractions

SRB 32–34

Study Link 4.9

Rename each decimal as a percent.

1. 0.65 = _____

2. 0.334 = _____

3. 0.02 = _____

4. 0.4 = _____

5. 2.7 = _____

6. 3.09 = _____

Rename each percent as a decimal.

7. 27% = _____

8. 53.9% = _____

9. 8% = _____

10. 60% = _____

11. 180% = _____

12. 115% = _____

Use division to rename each fraction as a decimal to the nearest hundredth.
Then rename the decimal as a percent.

13. $\frac{7}{8}$ = 0._____ = _____%

14. $\frac{3}{7}$ = 0._____ = _____%

15. $\frac{5}{12}$ = 0._____ = _____%

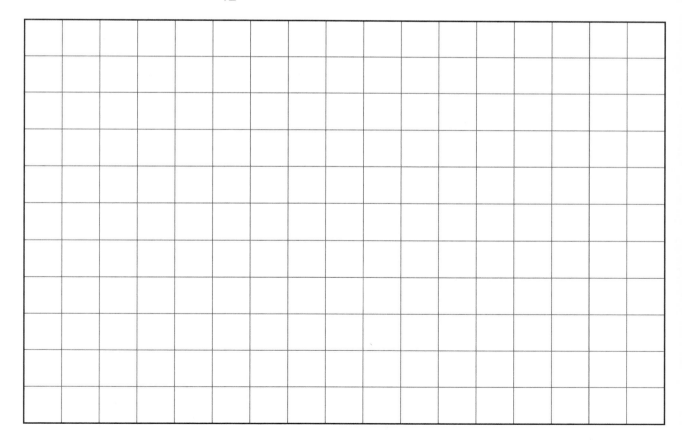

Circle Graphs

Use estimation to display the data in each problem in a circle graph. (*Hint:* For each percent, think of a simple fraction that is close to the value of the percent. Then estimate the size of the sector for each percent.) Remember to graph the smallest sector first.

1. In 1997, 13% of Americans were 65 or older, 61% were 19–64 years old, and 26% were 18 or younger.

2. 98% of households in the United States have at least one television.

3. In 1999, 69.8 million people were enrolled in school in the United States. 22.2% were college students, 21.9% were in Grades 9–12, and 55.9% were in Grades pre-K–8.

4. In 1997, NASA's total budget was $13.8 billion. 19% was spent on Mission Support, such as safety testing and facility construction. 39% was spent on Human Space Flight, such as the space shuttle. 42% was spent on Science, Aeronautics, and Technology, such as academic programs and research.

Source: Scholastic Kid's Almanac for the 21st Century

Percent Problems

  Study Link 4.11

The results of a survey about school children's weekly allowances are shown at the right.

Amount of Allowance	Percent of Children
$0	30%
$1–$4	20%
$5	25%
$6 or more	25%

1. Lincoln School has about 500 students. Use the survey results above to complete this table.

Amount of Allowance	Predicted Number of Students at Lincoln
$0	
$1–$4	
$5	
$6 or more	

2. The sixth grade at Lincoln has about 60 students. Use the survey results above to complete this table.

Amount of Allowance	Predicted Number of Sixth Grade Students at Lincoln
$0	
$1–$4	
$5	
$6 or more	

3. A rule of thumb for changing a number of meters to yards is to add the number of meters to 10% of the number of meters.

Examples 5 m is about 5 + (10% of 5), or 5.5 yd
10 m is about 10 + (10% of 10), or 11 yd

Use this rule of thumb to estimate how many yards are in the following numbers of meters.

a. 3 m is about 3 + (10% of 3), or _____ yd

b. 8 m is about 8 + (10% of 8), or _____ yd

c. 20 m is about 20 + (10% of 20), or _____ yd

Family Letter

Unit 5: Geometry: Congruence, Constructions, and Parallel Lines

In *Fourth* and *Fifth Grade Everyday Mathematics*, students used a compass and straightedge to construct basic shapes and create geometric designs. In Unit 5 of *Sixth Grade Everyday Mathematics*, students will review some basic construction techniques and then devise their own methods for copying triangles and quadrilaterals and for constructing parallelograms. The term **congruent** will be applied to their copies of line segments, angles, and 2-dimensional figures. Two figures are congruent if they have the *same size* and the *same shape.*

Another approach to congruent figures in Unit 5 is through isometry transformations. These are motions that take a figure from one place to another while preserving its size and shape. Reflections (flips), translations (slides), and rotations (turns) are basic isometry transformations (also known as rigid motions). A figure produced by an isometry transformation (the image) is congruent to the original figure (the preimage).

flip   slide   turn

Students will continue to work with the Geometry Template, a tool that was introduced in *Fifth Grade Everyday Mathematics*. The Geometry Template contains protractors and rulers for measuring, and cutouts for drawing geometric figures. The class will review how to measure and draw angles using both the full-circle and half-circle protractors.

Students will also use a protractor to construct circle graphs that represent data collections. This involves converting the data to percents of a total, finding the corresponding degree measures around a circle, and drawing sectors of the appropriate size.

Often, measures can be determined without use of a measuring tool. Students will apply properties of angles and sums of angles to find unknown measures in figures like the ones at the right.

One lesson in Unit 5 is a review and extension of work with the coordinate grid. Students will plot and name points on a four-quadrant coordinate grid and use the grid for further study of geometric shapes.

Please keep this Family Letter for reference as your child works through Unit 5.

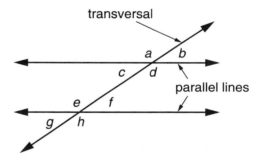

If the measure of any one angle is given, the measures of all the others can be found without measuring.

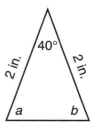

The sum of the angles in a triangle is 180°. Angles *a* and *b* have the same measure, 70°.

Math Tools

Your child will use a **compass** and **straightedge** to construct geometric figures. You might find that your child needs to practice making circles with a compass. A straightedge is only meant to be used to draw straight lines, not for measuring. The primary difference between a compass-and-straightedge construction and a drawing or sketch of a geometric figure is that measuring is *not* allowed in constructions.

Vocabulary

Important terms in Unit 5:

adjacent angles Angles that are next to each other; adjacent angles have a common side, but no other overlap. In the diagram, angles *a* and *b* are adjacent angles. So are angles *b* and *c*, and so on.

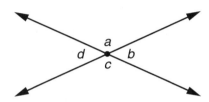

congruent Having exactly the same size and shape. Congruent figures are said to be *congruent to* each other.

ordered number pair Two numbers that are used to locate a point on a coordinate grid. The first number tells the position along the horizontal axis, and the second number gives the position along the vertical axis. Ordered pairs are usually written inside parentheses, for example, (2,3).

reflection (flip) The "flipping" of a figure over a line (line of reflection) so that its image is the mirror image of the original.

reflex angle An angle with a measure between 180° and 360°.

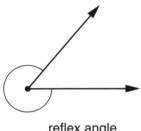

reflex angle

rotation (turn) A movement of a figure around a fixed point or axis; a "turn."

supplementary angles Two angles whose measures total 180°.

translation (slide) A movement of a figure along a straight line; a "slide."

vertical (opposite) angles When two lines intersect, the angles that do not share a common side. Vertical angles have equal measures. In the diagram, angles 1 and 3 are vertical angles. They have no sides in common. Similarly, angles 4 and 2 are vertical angles.

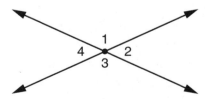

Use with Lesson 4.12.

Do-Anytime Activities

To work with your child on the concepts taught in this unit, try these interesting and rewarding activities:

1 While you are driving in the car together, have your son or daughter look for congruent figures: for example, windows in office buildings, circles on stop lights, and many street signs are all congruent figures.

2 Look for apparent right angles, or any other type of angles: acute (less than 90°), obtuse (between 90° and 180°). Guide your child to look particularly at bridge supports for a variety of angles.

3 Triangulation lends strength to furniture. Encourage your child to find corner, triangular braces in furniture throughout your home. Look under tables, under chairs, inside cabinets, or under bed frames. Have your child count how many instances of triangulation he or she can find in your home.

Building Skills through Games

In this unit, your child will work on his or her skills in measuring angles and using a coordinate grid by playing the following games. For detailed instructions, see the *Student Reference Book.*

Angle Tangle See *Student Reference Book,* page 278

Two players will need a protractor, straightedge, and blank paper to play *Angle Tangle.* Skills practiced include estimating angle measures as well as measuring angles.

Hidden Treasure See *Student Reference Book,* page 296

Hidden Treasure provides practice in using a coordinate grid (reference frames) and in developing strategies. Two players need a pencil, a red pen or crayon, and a gameboard for each player to play the game.

As You Help Your Child with Homework

As your child brings assignments home, you may want to go over the instructions together, clarifying them as necessary. The answers listed below will guide you through some of this unit's Study Links.

Study Link 5.1

2. **a.** ∠H **b.** ∠IJK

   c. ∠D **d.** ∠ABC, ∠EFG, ∠L

3. About 180° **4.** About 360°

Study Link 5.2

1. m∠y = 120°

2. m∠x = 115°

3. m∠c = 135° m∠a = 45° m∠t = 135°

4. m∠q = 120° m∠r = 80° m∠s = 70°

5. m∠a = 120° m∠b = 60° m∠c = 120°

   m∠d = 40° m∠e = 140° m∠f = 140°

   m∠g = 80° m∠h = 100° m∠i = 100°

6. m∠w = 90° m∠a = 75° m∠t = 105°

   m∠c = 75° m∠h = 105°

Study Link 5.3

1. **a.**

Age	Percent of Listeners	Degree Measure
18–24	11%	40°
25–34	18%	65°
35–44	24%	86°
45–54	20%	72°
55–64	11%	40°
65+	16%	58°

2. **a.** 1,920,000 adults **b.** 3,760,000 adults

Study Link 5.4

Sample answers for 1–3:

1. Vertex C: (1, 2)

2. Vertex F: (5, 10) Vertex G: (3, 7)

3. Vertex J: (2, 1) **4.** Vertex M: (−2, −3)

5. Vertex Q: (8, −3)

Study Link 5.5

1.   2. 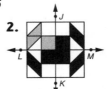 3.

Study Link 5.7

1. m∠r = 47° m∠s = 133° m∠t = 47°

2. m∠a = 120° m∠b = 120° m∠c = 60°

3. m∠x = 45° m∠y = 45° m∠z = 135°

4. m∠NKO = 10°

5. m∠c = 114° m∠a = 57° m∠t = 57°

6. m∠p = 54°

Study Link 5.8

2. A′: (−2, −7) B′: (−6, −6)
   C′: (−8, −4) D′: (−5, −1)

3. A″: (2, 1) B″: (6, 2)
   C″: (8, 4) B″: (5, 7)

4. A‴: (1, −2) D″: (2, −6)
   C‴: (4, −8) D‴: (7, −5)

Study Link 5.9

3. Sample answers: All of the vertical angles have the same measure; all of the angles along the transversal and on the same side are supplementary; opposite angles along the transversal are equal in measure.

Study Link 5.10

1. **a.** 50°; ∠YZW plus the 130° angle equal 180°; so ∠YZW = 50°. Since opposite angles in a parallelogram are equal, ∠X also equals 50°.

   b. 130°; Since ∠YZW = 50°; and it is a consecutive angle with ∠Y, and since consecutive angles of parallelograms are supplementary, ∠Y = 130°.

2. Opposite sides of a parallelogram are congruent.

3. 110°; Angles with a common side that form a straight line are supplementary.

4. square **5.** rhombus

Angles

1. Measure each angle. Write the measure next to the angle.

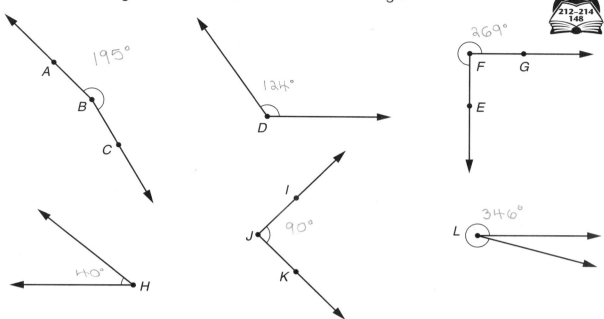

SRB
212–214
148

195°

124°

269°

90°

346°

2. a. Which of the above is an acute angle? _H_

b. A right angle? _J_

c. An obtuse angle? _D_

d. Which of the above are reflex angles? _B, F, L_

3. Use a ruler to draw a large triangle in the space at the right. Measure each angle. What is the sum of the three measures?

_____

4. Use a ruler to draw a large quadrangle in the space at the right. Measure each angle. What is the sum of the four measures?

_____

Angle Relationships

Find the following angle measures. Do *not* use a protractor.

SRB
151 215

1.

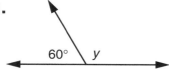

m ∠y = _____

2.

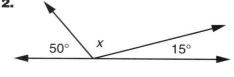

m ∠x = _____

3.

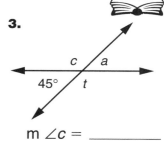

m ∠c = _____

m ∠a = _____

m ∠t = _____

4. m ∠q = _____

m ∠r = _____

m ∠s = _____

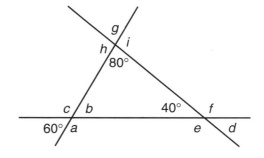

5. m ∠a = _____   m ∠b = _____

m ∠c = _____   m ∠d = _____

m ∠e = _____   m ∠f = _____

m ∠g = _____   m ∠h = _____

m ∠i = _____

6. m ∠w = _____   m ∠a = _____

m ∠t = _____   m ∠c = _____

m ∠h = _____

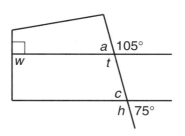

Circle Graphs

1. The table below shows a breakdown, by age group, of adults who listen to classical music.

   a. Calculate the degree measure of each sector to the nearest degree.

   b. Use a protractor to make a circle graph. Do *not* use the Percent Circle. Write a title for the graph.

Age	Percent of Listeners	Degree Measure
18–24	11%	
25–34	18%	
35–44	24%	
45–54	20%	
55–64	11%	
65+	16%	

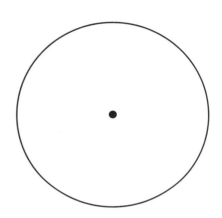

Source: USA Today, Snapshot

2. On average, about 8 million adults listen to classical music on the radio each day.

   a. Estimate how many adults between the ages of 35 and 44 listen to classical music on the radio each day.

   About _____
   (unit)

   b. Estimate how many adults at least 45 years old listen to classical music on the radio each day.

   About _____
   (unit)

More Polygons on a Coordinate Grid

For each polygon described below, some vertices are plotted on the grid. One or two vertices are missing.

SRB
154 157
216

- Plot and label the missing vertex or vertices on the grid. (There may be more than one place you can plot a point.)
- Write an ordered number pair for each vertex you plot.
- Draw the polygon.

1. Right triangle *ABC*   Vertex *C:* (____,____)

2. Parallelogram *DEFG*   Vertex *F:* (____,____)   Vertex *G:* (____,____)

3. Scalene triangle *HIJ*   Vertex *J:* (____,____)

4. Kite *KLMN*   Vertex *M:* (____,____)   **5.** Square *PQRS*   Vertex *Q:* (____,____)

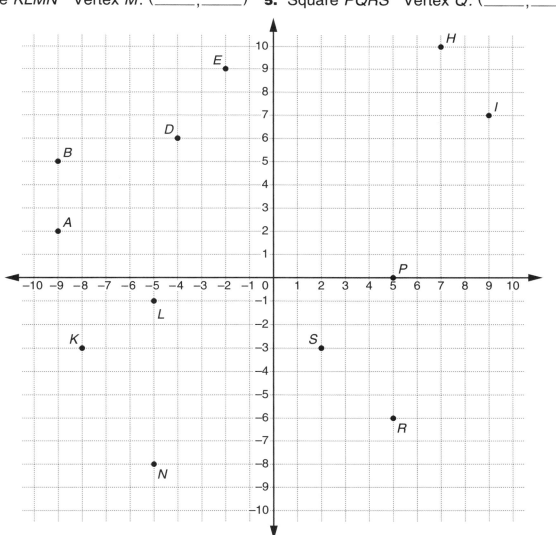

Transforming Patterns

A pattern can be translated, reflected, or rotated to create many different designs. Consider the pattern at the right.

The following examples show how the pattern can be transformed to create different designs:

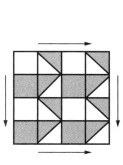
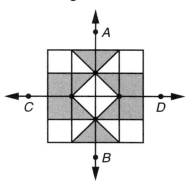
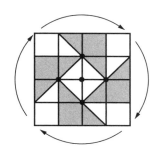

Translations   Reflections   Rotations

1. Translate the pattern at the right across two grid squares. Then translate the resulting pattern (the given pattern and its translation) down two grid squares.

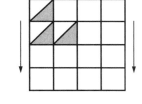

2. Reflect the given pattern over line *JK*. Reflect the resulting pattern (the given pattern and its reflection) over line *LM*.

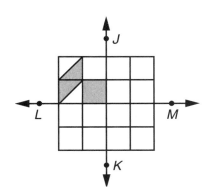

3. Rotate the given pattern clockwise 90° around point *X*. Repeat two more times.

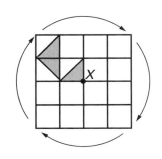

Congruent Figures and Copying

Column 1 below shows paths with the Start points marked. Complete each path in Column 2 so that it is congruent to the path in Column 1. Use the Start points marked in Column 2. In Problems 2 and 3, the copy will not be in the same position as the original path.

(*Hint:* If you have trouble, try tracing the path in Column 1 and then sliding, flipping, or rotating it so that its starting point matches the starting point in Column 2.)

Example These two paths are congruent, but they are not in the same position.

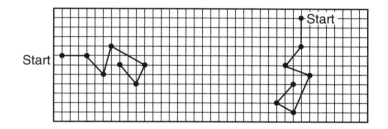

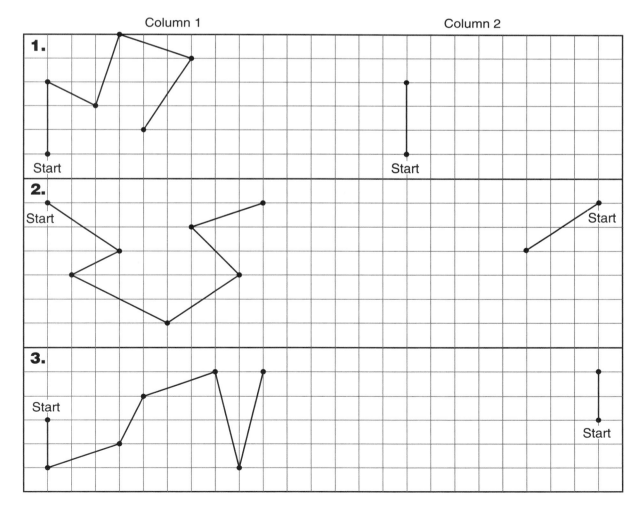

Angle Relationships

Write the measures of the angles indicated in Problems 1–6.
Do *not* use a protractor.

1.

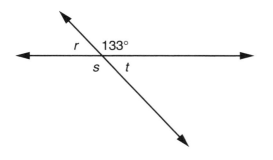

m ∠s = _____

m ∠r = _____

m ∠t = _____

2.

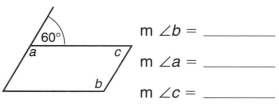

m ∠b = _____

m ∠a = _____

m ∠c = _____

3. Angles *x* and *y* have the same measure.

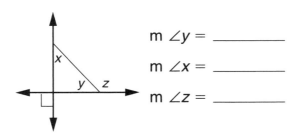

m ∠y = _____

m ∠x = _____

m ∠z = _____

4. ∠JKL is a straight angle.

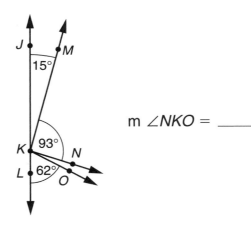

m ∠NKO = _____

5. Angles *a* and *t* have the same measure.

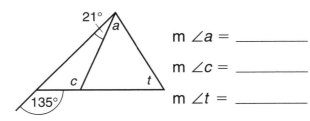

m ∠a = _____

m ∠c = _____

m ∠t = _____

6.

m ∠p = _____

Isometry Transformations on a Grid

1. Graph and label the following points on the coordinate grid. Connect the points in order to form quadrangle *ABCD*.

   A: (−2,1)
   B: (−6,2)
   C: (−8,4)
   D: (−5,7)

2. To slide quadrangle *ABCD,* subtract 8 from the second coordinate of each ordered pair in Problem 1. Plot and connect the new points. Label them *A'*, *B'*, *C'*, and *D'*.

   Record the new points.

   _____

   _____

   _____

   _____

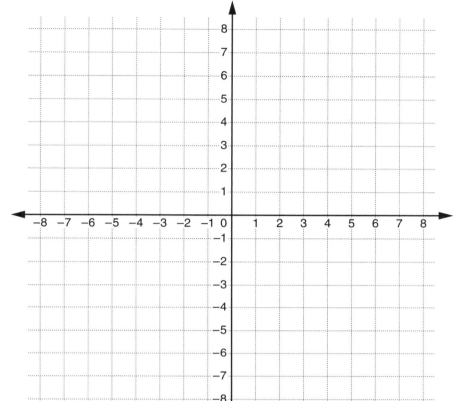

3. Reflect quadrangle *ABCD* across the *y*-axis. Plot and connect the new points. Label them *A''*, *B''*, *C''*, and *D''*.

   Record the new points.

   _____ _____ _____ _____

Challenge

4. Rotate quadrangle *A''B''C''D''* 90° clockwise around point (0,0). Plot and connect the new points. Label them *A'''*, *B'''*, *C'''*, and *D'''*.

   Record the new points.

   _____ _____ _____ _____

Parallel Lines and a Transversal

1. Use a ruler and straightedge to draw two parallel lines. Then draw another line that crosses both parallel lines.

2. Measure the eight angles in your figure. Write each measure inside the angle.

3. What patterns do you notice in your angle measures?

_____

_____

_____

_____

_____

_____

_____

_____

_____

Parallelogram Problems

All of the figures on this page are parallelograms. Do *not* use a ruler or protractor to solve Problems 1, 2, or 3.

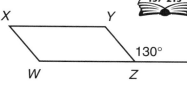

1. a. The measure of $\angle X =$ _____ °. Explain.

_____

_____

_____

_____

b. The measure of $\angle Y =$ _____ °. Explain.

_____

_____

_____

_____

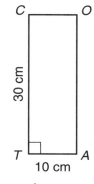

2. Alexi said that the only way to find the length of sides *CO* and *OA* is to measure them with a ruler. Explain why he is incorrect.

_____

_____

_____

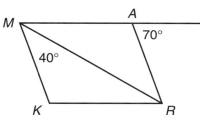

3. What is the measure of $\angle MAR$? _____ Explain.

_____

_____

4. Draw a parallelogram in which all sides have the same length and all angles have the same measure.

What is another name for this parallelogram? _____

5. Draw a parallelogram in which all sides have the same length and no angle measures 90°.

What is another name for this parallelogram? _____

Family Letter

Unit 6: Number Systems and Algebra Concepts

In *Fourth* and *Fifth Grade Everyday Mathematics*, your child worked with addition and subtraction of positive and negative numbers. In this unit, students use multiplication patterns to help them establish the rules for multiplying and dividing with positive and negative numbers. They also develop and use an algorithm for the division of fractions.

In the rest of the unit, your child will explore beginning algebra concepts. First, the class reviews how to determine whether a number sentence is true or false. This involves understanding what to do with numbers that are grouped within parentheses and knowing in what order to calculate if the groupings of numbers are not made explicit by parentheses.

Students then solve simple equations by trial and error to reinforce what it means to solve an equation—to replace a variable with a number that will make the number sentence true.

Next, they solve pan-balance problems, first introduced in *Fifth Grade Everyday Mathematics,* to develop a more systematic approach to solving equations. For example, to find out how many marbles weigh as much as 1 orange in the top balance at the right, you can first remove 1 orange from each pan and then remove half the remaining oranges from the left side and half the marbles from the right side. The pans will still balance.

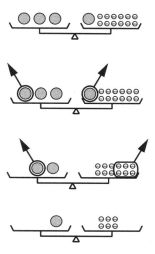

Students learn that each step in the solution of a pan-balance problem can be represented by an equation, thus leading to the solution of the original equation. You might ask your child to demonstrate how pan-balance problems work.

Finally, your child will learn how to solve inequalities— number sentences that compare two quantities that are not equal.

Please keep this Family Letter for reference as your child works through Unit 6.

Vocabulary

Important terms in Unit 6:

cover-up method A method for solving equations by covering up key expressions.

Division of Fractions property The principle says that division by a fraction is equivalent to multiplication by the fraction's reciprocal. For example, since the reciprocal of $\frac{1}{2}$ is 2, the division problem $4 / \frac{1}{2}$ is equivalent to the multiplication problem $4 * 2$.

integers A number in the set $\{..., -4, -3, -2, -1, 0, 1, 2, 3, 4, ...\}$; a whole number or the opposite of a whole number.

multiplication property of -1 A property of multiplication that says that for any number a, $(-1) * a = (OPP) a$, or $-a$.
For example, for a = 5: $5 * (-1) = (OPP)5 = -5$.
For $a = -3$: $-3 * -1 = (OPP)-3 = -(-3) = 3$.

opposite of a number A number that is the same distance from zero on the number line as a given number, but on the opposite side of zero. For example, the opposite of $+3$ is -3 and the opposite of -5 is $+5$.

order of operations Rules that tell in what order to perform operations. The order of operations is
1. Do the operations in parentheses first. (Use rules 2–4 inside the parentheses.)
2. Calculate all the expressions with exponents.
3. Multiply and divide in order, from left to right.
4. Add and subtract in order from left to right.

reciprocals Two numbers whose product is 1. Not all reciprocals are expressed as fractions; for example, 2 is the reciprocal of $\frac{1}{2}$ because $2 * \frac{1}{2} = 1$.

relation symbol A symbol used to express a relationship between two quantities: $=$ (is equal to); $\neq$ (is not equal to); $>$ (is greater than); $\geq$ (is greater than or equal to); $<$ (is less than); $\leq$ (is less than or equal to).

trial-and-error method A method for finding the solution to an equation by trying several test numbers.

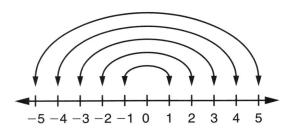

Use with Lesson 5.11.

Do-Anytime Activities

To work with your child on the concepts taught in this unit and in previous units, try these interesting and rewarding activities:

1 If your child helps with dinner, ask him or her to identify uses of positive and negative numbers in the kitchen. For example, negative numbers might be used to describe the temperature in the freezer, and positive numbers are used to measure liquid and dry ingredients. For a quick game, you might imagine a vertical number line with the countertop as 0; everything above is referenced by a positive number, and everything below it is represented by a negative number. Give your child directions for getting out such items as this: "the -2 mixing bowl"; that is, the bowl on the second shelf below the counter.

2 If your child needs extra practice adding and subtracting positive and negative numbers, ask him or her to bring home the directions for the *Credits/Debits Game.* Play a few rounds for review.

3 For dinner conversation, after Lesson 6, ask your child to explain to you what this sentence means: Please Excuse My Dear Aunt Sally. If he or she doesn't know, offer the reminder that it is a memory device. It is the rule for the order of operations: parentheses, exponents, multiplication, division, addition, subtraction. The family might enjoy inventing another sentence with the same initial letters: Perhaps Everything Might Drop Again Soon; Poignant Elopements Might Develop After Sunset.

Recording Sheet			
	Start	Change	End/next start
1	$+\$10$		
2			
3			
4			
5			
6			
7			
8			
9			
10			

Building Skills Through Games

In this unit, your child will work on their understanding of equations, as well as addition, subtraction, multiplication, and division facts by playing the following games. For detailed instructions, see the *Student Reference Book.*

Algebra Election See *Student Reference Book,* pages 276 and 277

Two teams of two players will need 32 *Algebra Election* Problem Cards, an Electoral Vote map, 1 six-sided die, 4 pennies or other small counters, and a calculator to play. This game provides the student practice with solving equations.

Credits/Debits Game See *Student Reference Book,* page 282

Two players use a complete deck of number cards and recording sheet to play *Credits/Debits.* Playing *Credits/Debits* helps students practice adding and subtracting positive and negative numbers.

Top-It See *Student Reference Book,* pages 308 and 309

Top-It games provide practice with basic addition, subtraction, multiplication and division facts. One or more players need number cards 0–9, 4 of each card, and a calculator to play *Top-It* games.

As You Help Your Child with Homework

As your child brings assignments home, you may want to go over the instructions together, clarifying them as necessary. The answers listed below will guide you through this unit's Study Links.

Study Link 6.1

2. ✔   **3.** ✔   **5.** ✔

7. $\frac{1}{19}$ **8.** $2\frac{1}{2}$ **9.** $\frac{7}{26}$

10. 6   **11.** $2\frac{4}{5}$ **12.** $\frac{3}{4}$

13. $3\frac{35}{36}$ **14.** 1   **15.** $12\frac{1}{2}$ lb

16. $38\frac{1}{4}$ in.   **17.** $67\frac{1}{2}$ in.^{3}

Study Link 6.2

1. $\frac{2}{3} * \frac{6}{5} = \frac{12}{15} = \frac{4}{5}$

2. 1   **3.** 1   **4.** $5\frac{4}{9}$ **5.** 1

6. 8   **7.** $\frac{5}{98}$ **8.** $\frac{35}{36}$ **9.** $\frac{12}{35}$ **10.** $\frac{3}{10}$

11. Problems 1, 2, 3, 5, 9, and 10 should be circled.

12. 10 segments   **13.** 14 segments

14. 17 segments

Study Link 6.3

1. a. $46 + (-19) = 27$
   b. $-43 + (-17) = -60$
   c. $-5 + 6.8 = 1.8$
   d. $21 + 21 = 42$

2. a. -29 **b.** 43   **c.** $-2\frac{1}{5}$ **d.** 8.4
   e. $-3\frac{1}{4}$ **f.** $-\frac{1}{2}$ **g.** -18.2

3. a. (-2) **b.** 17   **c.** $2\frac{1}{4}$ **d.** $\frac{9}{10}$
   e. -3.7 **f.** (-146.2) **g.** $-\frac{7}{16}$

Study Link 6.4

1. -60 **2.** -9 **3.** -6 **4.** -6

5. -5 **6.** -240 **7.** -6 **8.** -28

9. $-1,150$ **10.** 162   **11.** -54 **12.** 2

13. -2 **14.** -360 **15.** $-\frac{5}{9}$ **16.** 48

17. -2 **18.** $1\frac{1}{2}$

19. a. 36   **b.** 77   **c.** -0.5 **d.** -16

Study Link 6.6

1. 21   **2.** 20   **3.** $\frac{21}{32}$ **4.** 43.4   **5.** 72

6. 33   **7.** 1   **8.** -15 **9.** 28   **10.** $-\frac{7}{10}$

Study Link 6.7

1. a. $17 < 27$; $3 * 15 < 100$; $(5 - 4) * 20 = 20$; $12 \neq 12$
   b. A number sentence must have a relation symbol.

2. a. true   **b.** false   **c.** false   **d.** true

3. a. $(28 - 6) + 9 = 31$ **b.** $20 < (40 - 9) + 11$
   c. $(36 / 6) / 2 < 12$ **d.** $4 * (8 - 4) = 16$

4. a. $60 - 14 = 50$; false   **b.** $90 = 3 * 30$; true
   c. $21 + 7 < 40$; true   **d.** $\sqrt{36} > \frac{1}{2} * 10$; true

Study Link 6.8

1. a. $b = 19$ **b.** $n = 24$ **c.** $x = 7$
   d. $k = \frac{4}{6}$ **e.** $y = 3$ **f.** $m = \frac{1}{5}$

2. a. $\frac{x}{6} = 10$; $x = 60$
   b. $200 - 7 = n$; $n = 193$
   c. $48 * b = 2,928$; $b = 61$
   d. $27 = 13 + n$; $n = 14$

3. Sample answers:
   a. $(3 * 11) + (12 - 9)$
   b. $2 * 18 + 14$
   c. $(10 * 3) + 15$
   d. $(17 - 5) + 14 - 4$
   e. $(20 + 14) + 7$

Study Link 6.9

1. 1   **2.** $1\frac{1}{2}$ **3.** 5   **4.** 1

Study Link 6.10

1. $k - 4 = 5$ **2.** Multiply by 2. M2
   $3k - 12 = 15$ Subtract 3q. S3q
   $20k - 12 = 15 + 17k$ Add 5. A5

Study Link 6.11

1. $k = 12$ **2.** $m = 5$

3. $x = 1$ **4.** $d = -6$

5. $r = 2$ **6.** $p = 5$

Practice with Fractions

Put a check mark next to each pair of equivalent fractions.

1. _____ $\frac{2}{3}$ and $\frac{5}{6}$

2. _____ $1\frac{3}{4}$ and $\frac{28}{16}$

3. _____ $\frac{24}{30}$ and $\frac{4}{5}$

4. _____ $\frac{7}{3}$ and $\frac{3}{7}$

5. _____ $\frac{56}{8}$ and $\frac{49}{7}$

6. _____ $2\frac{3}{8}$ and $\frac{19}{4}$

Find the reciprocal of each number. Check your answers with a calculator.

7. 19 _____

8. $\frac{2}{5}$ _____

9. $3\frac{5}{7}$ _____

10. $\frac{1}{6}$ _____

Multiply. Write your answers in simplest form. Show your work.

11. $\frac{2}{5} * 7 =$ _____

12. $\frac{2}{3} * 1\frac{1}{8} =$ _____

13. $2\frac{1}{6} * 1\frac{5}{6} =$ _____

14. $3\frac{1}{7} * \frac{7}{22} =$ _____

Solve the number stories.

15. How much does a box containing 5 horseshoes weigh, if each horseshoe weighs about $2\frac{1}{2}$ pounds? _____

16. One and a half dozen golf tees are laid in a straight line, end to end. If each tee is $2\frac{1}{8}$ inches long, how long is the line of tees? _____

17. A standard-size brick is 8 inches long and $2\frac{1}{4}$ inches high and has a depth of $3\frac{3}{4}$ inches. What is the volume of a standard-size brick? _____

Fraction Division

Division of Fractions Algorithm

$$\frac{a}{b} \div \frac{c}{d} = \frac{a}{b} * \frac{d}{c}$$

Divide. Show your work.

1. $\frac{2}{3} \div \frac{5}{6} =$ _____

2. $1\frac{3}{4} \div \frac{28}{16} =$ _____

3. $\frac{24}{30} \div \frac{4}{5} =$ _____

4. $\frac{7}{3} \div \frac{3}{7} =$ _____

5. $\frac{5}{8} \div \frac{5}{8} =$ _____

6. $2 \div \frac{1}{4} =$ _____

7. $\frac{1}{7} \div 2\frac{4}{5} =$ _____

8. $5\frac{5}{6} \div 6 =$ _____

9. $\frac{3}{4} \div 2\frac{3}{16} =$ _____

10. $1\frac{1}{5} \div \frac{12}{3} =$ _____

11. Circle the problems above that are easiest to solve using a common denominator.

Challenge

12. How many $\frac{3}{10}$ centimeter segments are in 3 centimeters? _____ segments

13. How many $\frac{3}{10}$ centimeter segments are in $4\frac{1}{5}$ centimeters? _____ segments

14. How many $\frac{4}{10}$ centimeter segments are in $6\frac{4}{5}$ centimeters? _____ segments

Subtraction of Positive and Negative Numbers Study Link 6.3

To subtract *b* from *a*, add the opposite of *b* to *a*. For any numbers *a* and *b*,
$a - b = a + (OPP)\, b$, or $a - b = a + (-b)$.

1. Rewrite each subtraction problem as an addition problem. Then solve
   the problem.

   a. $46 - 19 =$ _____

   b. $-43 - 17 =$ _____

   c. $-5 - (-6.8) =$ _____

   d. $21 - (-21) =$ _____

2. Subtract.

   a. $-72 - (-43) =$ _____

   b. _____ $= 4 - (-39)$

   c. $-\left(\frac{7}{10}\right) - 1\frac{1}{2} =$ _____

   d. $4.8 - (-3.6) =$ _____

   e. _____ $= -2\frac{1}{2} - \frac{3}{4}$

   f. $-\left(\frac{5}{6}\right) - \left(-\frac{1}{3}\right) =$ _____

   g. $-12.3 - 5.9 =$ _____

   h. $-8.5 - (-2.7) =$ _____

3. Fill in the missing numbers.

   a. $19 = 17 -$ _____

   b. $-43 = -26 -$ _____

   c. $\frac{1}{2} -$ _____ $= -1\frac{3}{4}$

   d. _____ $- \left(-2\frac{4}{5}\right) = 3\frac{7}{10}$

   e. $-17.6 =$ _____ $- 13.9$

   f. $83.5 = -62.7 -$ _____

   g. _____ $= 5\frac{3}{4} - 6\frac{3}{16}$

   h. $9.6 -$ _____ $= 10$

∗, / of Positive and Negative Numbers

SRB
95

Multiplication Property	**Division Property**
For all numbers a and b, if the values of a and b are both positive or both negative, then the product $a ∗ b$ is a positive number. If one of the values is positive and the other is negative, then the product $a ∗ b$ is a negative number.	For all numbers a and b, if the values of a and b are both positive or both negative, then the quotient a / b is a positive number. If one of the values is positive and the other is negative, then the quotient a / b is a negative number.

Solve. Use a calculator to check your answers.

1. $-12 ∗ 5 =$ _____

2. $-63 / 7 =$ _____

3. $24 ÷ (-4) =$ _____

4. $-9 ∗$ _____ $= 54$

5. $-50 /$ _____ $= 10$

6. $-6 ∗ 5 ∗ 8 =$ _____

7. $48 / (-6 - 2) =$ _____

8. $(-8 ∗ 5) + 12 =$ _____

9. $50 ∗ (-23) =$ _____

10. $6 ∗ (12 + 15) =$ _____

11. $(-90 ÷ 10) + (-45) =$ _____

12. $56 / (-7) / (-4) =$ _____

13. _____ $∗ (-7) ∗ (-4) = -56$

14. _____ $÷ 40 = -9$

Challenge

15. $\frac{2}{3} ∗ \left(-\frac{5}{6}\right) =$ _____

16. $(8 ∗ (-3)) - (8 ∗ (-9)) =$ _____

17. $0.25 ∗ (-8) =$ _____

18. $\left(-\frac{3}{4}\right) ÷ \left(-\frac{1}{2}\right) =$ _____

19. Evaluate each expression for $b = -7$.

    a. $(-9 ∗ b) - 27 =$ _____

    b. $11 ∗ (-b) =$ _____

    c. $-b / (-14) =$ _____

    d. $b - (b + 16) =$ _____

Turn-Around Patterns

SRB
94

Fill in the missing numbers in the tables. Look for patterns in the results.

1.

x	y	(OPP) x	(OPP) y	x + y	y + x	x − y	y − x
7	9	−7	−9	16			
−2	12						
−3	−9						
$\frac{2}{3}$	$\frac{5}{6}$						
2.7	−1.9						
2^2	2^3						

Which patterns did you find in your completed table?

_____

_____

_____

2.

x	y	$\frac{1}{x}$	$\frac{1}{y}$	x * y	y * x	x ÷ y	y ÷ x
7	9	$\frac{1}{7}$	$\frac{1}{9}$	63			
−2	12						
−3	−9						
$\frac{2}{3}$	$\frac{5}{6}$						
2.7	−1.9						
2^2	2^3						

Which patterns did you find in your completed table?

_____

_____

_____

Using Order of Operations

> Please Excuse My Dear Aunt Sally
>
> Parentheses Exponents Multiplication Division Addition Subtraction

Evaluate each expression.

1. $5 + 6 * 3 - 2 =$ _____

2. $4 * 9 / 2 + (-4 + 6) =$ _____

3. $\frac{1}{2} + \frac{5}{8} * \frac{1}{2} \div 2 =$ _____

4. $(2.3 + 7.8) * 4 + 3 =$ _____

5. $4^2 + 7(3 - (-5)) =$ _____

6. $((2 * 4) + 3) * 6 / 2 =$ _____

Evaluate the following expressions for $m = -3$.

7. $-\frac{m}{m} + 6 - 4 =$ _____

8. $((4 + 11) * -3) / 9 * (-m) =$ _____

9. $m^2 + (-(m^3)) - 8 =$ _____

10. $\frac{1}{2} * m \div \frac{5}{4} + \frac{3}{5} - \frac{1}{10} =$ _____

Number Sentences

1. a. Draw a circle around each number sentence.

$17 < 27$ $3 * 15 < 100$ $56 / 8$

$(5 - 4) * 20 = 20$ $(4 + 23) / 9$ $12 \neq 12$

b. Choose one item that you did not circle. Explain why it is not a number sentence.

_____

_____

2. Tell whether each number sentence is true or false.

a. $9 - (6 + 2) > 0.5$ _____   **b.** $94 = 49 - 2 * 2$ _____

c. $\frac{24}{6} < 33 / 11$ _____   **d.** $70 - 25 = 45$ _____

3. Insert parentheses so that each number sentence is true.

a. $28 - 6 + 9 = 31$ **b.** $20 < 40 - 9 + 11$

c. $36 / 6 / 2 < 12$ **d.** $4 * 8 - 4 = 16$

4. Write a number sentence for each word sentence. Tell whether the number sentence is true or false.

Word sentence	Number sentence	True or false?
a. If 14 is subtracted from 60, the result is 50.	_____	_____
b. 90 is three times as much as 30.	_____	_____
c. 21 increased by 7 is less than 40.	_____	_____
d. The square root of 36 is greater than half of 10.	_____	_____

Solving Simple Equations

1. Find the solution to each equation.

   a. $b - 7 = 12$ _____   **b.** $53 = n + 29$ _____

   c. $x = 63 / 9$ _____   **d.** $\frac{1}{2} * k = \frac{4}{12}$ _____

   e. $45 / y^2 = 5$ _____   **f.** $m * \frac{2}{3} = 1 - \frac{13}{15}$ _____

2. Translate the English sentences below into equations. Then find the solution to each equation.

English sentence	Equation	Solution
a. If you divide a number by 6, the result is 10.	_____	_____
b. Which number is 7 less than 200?	_____	_____
c. A number multiplied by 48 is equal to 2,928.	_____	_____
d. 27 is equal to 13 increased by which number?	_____	_____

3. For each problem, use parentheses and as many numbers and operations as you can to write an expression equal to the target number. You may use each number just once in an expression. For example, for Problem 3a, you can write the expression 3 * 12. Try to write expressions with more than two numbers.

   a. Numbers: 3, 9, 11, 12, 19   Target number: 36 _____

   b. Numbers: 1, 2, 6, 14, 18   Target number: 50 _____

   c. Numbers: 3, 9, 10, 15, 16   Target number: 45 _____

   d. Numbers: 4, 5, 8, 14, 17   Target number: 22 _____

   e. Numbers: 6, 7, 12, 14, 20   Target number: 41 _____

Solving Pan-Balance Problems

Solve these pan-balance problems. In each diagram, the two pans are balanced.

1. One ball weighs

as much as _____ coin(s).

2. One cube weighs

as much as _____ marble(s).

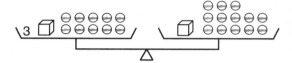

3. One *X* weighs

as much as _____ *Y*(s).

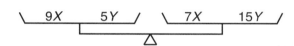

4. One *A* weighs

as much as _____ *B*(s).

Make up two pan-balance problems for someone in your class to solve.

5.

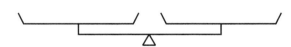

_____

_____

6.

_____

_____

Balancing Equations

For Problem 1, record the result of each operation on each pan.

1. Original pan-balance equation

Operation	
(in words)	**(abbreviation)**
Subtract 4.	S 4
Multiply by 3.	M 3
Add 17k.	A 17k

$$k = 9$$

$$\underline{\hspace{3cm}} = \underline{\hspace{3cm}}$$

$$\underline{\hspace{3cm}} = \underline{\hspace{3cm}}$$

$$\underline{\hspace{3cm}} = \underline{\hspace{3cm}}$$

For Problems 2 and 3, record the operation that was used to obtain the result on each pan balance.

2. Original pan-balance equation

Operation	
(in words)	**(abbreviation)**
_____	_____
_____	_____
_____	_____

$$1 + 1.5q = 2q - 2.5$$

$$2 + 3q = 4q - 5$$

$$2 = q - 5$$

$$7 = q$$

3. Original pan-balance equation

Operation	
(in words)	**(abbreviation)**
_____	_____
_____	_____
_____	_____

$$-3m + 12 = 13 - 5m$$

$$2m + 12 = 13$$

$$m + 6 = 6\frac{1}{2}$$

$$m = \frac{1}{2}$$

Solving Equations

Solve the equations. Check the solutions.

1. $9 + 5k = 45 + 2k$

Original equation

$$9 + 5k = 45 + 2k$$

Operation

S 9 $5k = 36 + 2k$

           $k = 12$

Check

2. $\frac{9}{2}m - 8 = -5.5 + 4m$

Original equation

Operation

Check

3. $24x - 10 = 18x - 4$

Original equation

Operation

Check

4. $12d - 9 = 15d + 9$

Original equation

Operation

Check

5. $-6r - 5 = 7 - 12r$

Original equation

Operation

Check

6. $\frac{1}{3}p + 7 = 12 - \frac{2}{3}p$

Original equation

Operation

Check

Review

1. Write an equation for each English statement.

English statement   Equation

a. Twice a number is 15. _____

b. 5 more than a number is 75. _____

c. 105 equals a number increased by 25. _____

d. Three times a number equals negative 240. _____

2. For which equation in Problem 1 is the solution 80? _____

3. The temperature was 12 degrees below zero. It dropped 15 degrees. What is the temperature now? Circle the equation you would use to solve the problem.

$$12 - 15 = T \qquad -12 + 15 = T \qquad -12 - 15 = T \qquad -12 - (-15) = T$$

4. Solve.

a. $-4 + 8 =$ _____   **b.** $-6 * (-5) =$ _____   **c.** $\frac{1}{2} * 3\frac{1}{4} =$ _____

d. $\frac{3}{4} \div \frac{1}{4} =$ _____   **e.** $1\frac{1}{2} \div \frac{1}{4} =$ _____   **f.** $-15 - (-3) =$ _____

5. Insert parentheses to make each equation true.

a. $9 * 6 + 4 = 90$ **b.** $2 * 7^2 = 9 * 12 - 10$

6. Follow the rules for order of operations to solve the problems.

a. $5 * 6 + 8 * 2 =$ _____   **b.** $20 - 8 / 2^2 =$ _____

c. $40 + 8 - 24 * 2 =$ _____   **d.** $4^3 / 2^5 =$ _____

7. Solve the equations.

a. $3x - 5 = 5x - 3$ **b.** $\dfrac{(4y + 5)}{2} = y + 9$

Solution _____   Solution _____

Family Letter

Unit 7: Probability and Discrete Mathematics

All of us are aware that the world is filled with uncertainties. As Ben Franklin wrote, "Nothing is certain except death and taxes!" Of course, there are some things we can be sure of: The sun will rise tomorrow, for example. We also know that there are degrees of uncertainty—some things are more likely to happen than others. There are occurrences that, although uncertain, can be predicted with reasonable accuracy.

While predictions are usually most reliable when they deal with general trends, it is possible and often helpful to predict the outcomes of specific situations. In Unit 7, your child will learn how to simulate a situation with random outcomes and how to determine the likelihood of various outcomes. Additionally, the class will analyze games of chance to determine whether or not they are fair—that is, whether or not all players have the same chance of winning.

We will be looking at two tools for analyzing probability situations—tree diagrams (familiar from single-elimination sports tournaments) and Venn diagrams (circle diagrams that show relationships between overlapping groups).

One lesson concerns strategies for taking multiple-choice tests based on probability. Should test takers guess at answers they don't know? Your child will learn some of the advantages and disadvantages of guessing on this type of test.

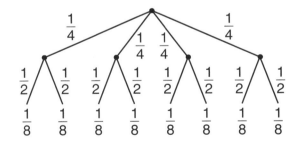

Tree diagram

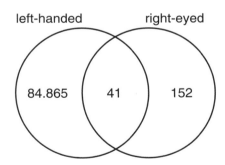

Venn diagram

Please keep this Family Letter for reference as your child works through Unit 7.

Vocabulary

Important terms in Unit 7:

equally likely Outcomes that have the same likelihood of happening.

expected outcome The average outcome over a large number of repetitions of a random experiment. For example, the expected outcome of rolling one die is the average number of spots showing over a large number of rolls.

outcome A possible result of a random process. For example, heads and tails are the two possible outcomes of tossing a coin.

probability A number between 0 and 1 that tells the chance that an event will happen. The closer a probability is to 1, the more likely the event is to happen.

probability tree diagram A drawing used to analyze the possible outcomes in a random situation. For example, the "leaves" of the probability tree diagram below represent the four equally likely outcomes when one coin is flipped two times.

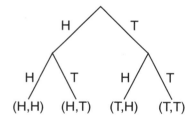

random number A number that has the same chance of appearing as any other number. Rolling a *fair* die will produce random numbers.

simulation A model of a real situation. For example, a fair coin can be used to simulate a series of games between two equally-matched teams.

Venn diagram A picture that uses circles to show relationships among sets. The Venn diagram below shows the number of students who have either a dog, a cat, or both.

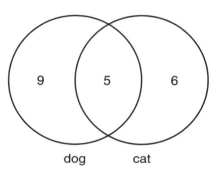

Use with Lesson 6.13.

Do-Anytime Activities

To work with your child on the concepts taught in this unit, try these interesting and rewarding activities:

1 While playing a game that uses a die, keep a tally sheet of how many times a certain number lands. For example, try to find out how many times during the game the number 5 comes up. Have your child write the probability for the chosen number. ($\frac{1}{6}$ is the probability that any given number on a six-sided die will land.) The tally sheet should show how many times the die was rolled during the game and how many times the chosen number came up.

2 Have your child listen to the weather forecast on television and pick out the language of probability. Have him or her listen for such terms as *likely, probability, (percent) chance, unlikely,* and so on.

3 Watch with your child for events that occur without dependence on any other event. In human relationships, truly independent events may be difficult to isolate, but this observation alone helps to define the randomness of events. Guide your child to see the difference between dependent events and independent events. For example, "Will Uncle Mike come for dinner?" depends on whether or not he got his car fixed. However, "Will I get heads or tails when I flip this coin?" depends on no other event.

Building Skills through Games

In this unit, your child will work on his or her understanding of estimation, measurement, and fractions by playing the following games. For more detailed instructions, see the *Student Reference Book.*

Angle Tangle See *Student Reference Book,* page 278
Two players need a protractor, straightedge, and blank sheets of paper to play this game. Mastering the estimation and measurement of angles is the goal of *Angle Tangle.*

Fraction Action, Fraction Friction See *Student Reference Book,* page 293
This is a game for 2 or 3 players. Game materials include one set of 16 *Fraction Action, Fraction Friction* cards and one or more calculators. Playing *Fraction Action, Fraction Friction* helps students review estimating sums of fractions.

Frac-Tac-Toe See *Student Reference Book,* pages 290–292
This is a game for 2 players. Game materials include 4 each of the number cards 0–10, pennies or other counters of two colors, a calculator, and a Gameboard. The Gameboard is a 5 by 5 number grid that resembles a bingo card. Several versions of the Gameboard are shown in the *Student Reference Book. Frac-Tac-Toe* helps students practice converting fractions to decimals and percents.

Name That Number See *Student Reference Book,* page 301
This game provides students with practice in naming numbers with number sentences. Two or three players need 1 complete deck of number cards to play *Name That Number.*

As You Help Your Child with Homework

As your child brings assignments home, you may want to go over the instructions together, clarifying them as necessary. The answers listed below will guide you through some of the Study Links in this unit.

Study Link 7.1

1. 1   **2.** 0, or 1   **3.** 0   **4.** 3

5. 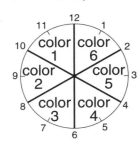   **6.**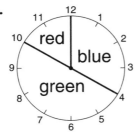

Study Link 7.2

1. no; Sample answer: Teams should be evenly matched. A team selected at random might not have a balance of skilled and unskilled players.

2. Yes and no; Sample answer: In an elementary school, preference for the better seats should go to the youngest children so that they can see the game. But starting in Grades 3 through 6, the principal should choose seat assignments randomly.

3. disagree; Sample answer: There is always an even chance of landing on black or white. The previous spins do not affect the outcome.

Study Link 7.3

2. Sample answer: The chance that a 6 will come up is $\frac{1}{6}$; therefore, the more the die is rolled, the more likely it is that a 6 will come up.

3. Sample answer: It is impossible to tell; Although the probability that a 6 will come up is 1 out of 6 times, in a small sample of actual trial results, the outcomes are nearly impossible to predict.

4. Sample answer: The chances of rolling a die so that a particular face comes up increases or decreases with the number of faces on the die.

Study Link 7.4

1. a. 115 people **b.** 185 people

2. a. 35 people **b.** 28 people **c.** 49 people

Study Link 7.5

1. There are 12 possible combinations: TON TOE PIE POE PON TAE TIN PAN TIE PAE PIN TAN

2. The probability of forming an English word is $\frac{8}{12}$, or $\frac{2}{3}$.

Study Link 7.6

1.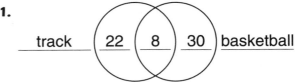

2. 60   **3.** 22   **4.** 30

5. 52   **6.** 30%   **7.** 11%

8. 15%   **9.** 4%   **10.** 70%

Study Link 7.7

1. a.   **c.**   **e.**   **g.**

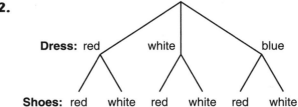

Study Link 7.8

2.

3. 6 combinations   **4.** $\frac{2}{6}$, or $\frac{1}{3}$

5.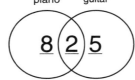

6. 5 students   **7.** $\frac{15}{25}$, or $\frac{3}{5}$

Blast from the Past

Third Grade

Color the blocks in the bags blue. How many red blocks would you put in each bag?

1. If I wanted to have an equal chance
of taking out red or blue, I would put in _____ red block(s).

2. If I wanted to be more likely to
take out blue than red, I could put in _____ red block(s).

3. If I wanted to be sure of taking
out a blue block, I would put in _____ red block(s).

4. If I wanted to take out a red block
about three times as often as
a blue one, I would put in _____ red block(s).

Fourth Grade

5. Make a spinner. Color the circle in six different colors so
that the spinner has the **same chance** of landing on
each color.

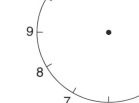

6. Make another spinner. Color the circle red, blue, and green
so that the spinner has

- a $\frac{1}{6}$ chance of landing on red, and

- a $\frac{1}{3}$ chance of landing on blue.

What fraction of the circle did you color

red? _____   blue? _____   green? _____

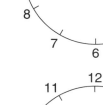

Fifth Grade

7. Draw a line from each of the spinners to the number that
best describes the chance of landing in the black area.

Chance of Landing on Black	$\frac{1}{10}$	0.25	50%	$\frac{2}{3}$	0.75	90%
Spinner						

Using Random Numbers

1. A gym teacher is dividing her class into two teams to play soccer.
Do you think she should choose the teams "at random"? _____

SRB
142

Explain. _____

_____

_____

2. The entire school is going to a baseball game.
Some seats are better than others.
Should the principal select the section
where each class will sit "at random"? _____

Explain. _____

_____

_____

_____

3. The spinner at the right has landed on the shaded part 5 times in a row.
Renee says, "On the next spin, the spinner is more likely to land on white
than on the shaded part."

Do you agree or disagree with Renee? _____

Explain. _____

_____

_____

4. The spinner at the right has landed on the shaded part 5 times in row.
Matthew says, "On the next spin, the spinner has a better chance of
landing on white than on the shaded part."

Do you agree or disagree with Matthew? _____

Explain. _____

_____

_____

_____

Probability Problems

1. Ron hates to decide what to wear. He made spinners to help him pick his clothes each day. The statements below describe his spinners. Draw spinners to match the statements. Label or color each section with the correct color.

Pants

He is twice as likely to wear his blue pants as his tan pants.

He will wear his black pants about $\frac{1}{4}$ of the time.

About 50% of the time, he will wear his blue pants.

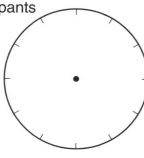

Pants

Shirts

He will wear his yellow shirt the least often.

He will wear his red shirt about half as often as his white shirt.

About $37\frac{1}{2}$% of the time, he will wear his blue shirt.

He will wear his white shirt about 1 out of every 3 times.

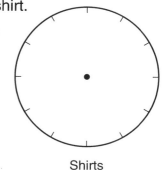

Shirts

Marlene played a game with a friend. The rules were, "Take turns rolling a die. The first player to roll a 6 wins." Marlene figured she would win if she let her friend roll first.

2. Why did Marlene think she would win if her friend rolled first?

_____

_____

_____

3. Do you think she won when her friend rolled first?

_____

Explain. _____

_____

_____

4. Explain how the game changes if the die does not have 6 sides. (There are dice with 4 sides, 8 sides, 12 sides, and 20 sides.)

_____

_____

_____

Tree Diagrams

SRB
143

Suppose you are walking through a maze. When the path divides, you randomly select the next path to follow. Each path has an equal chance of being selected. You may not retrace your steps. Depending on which paths you follow, you will end up in one room or another.

You may wish to make tree diagrams to help you solve the following problems.

1. Suppose 300 people take turns walking through the maze below.

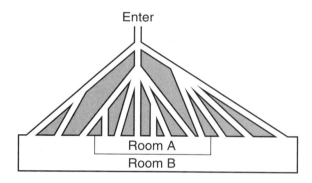

   a. About how many people would you expect to end up in Room A? _____

   b. About how many people would you expect to end up in Room B? _____

2. Suppose 112 people take turns walking through the maze below.

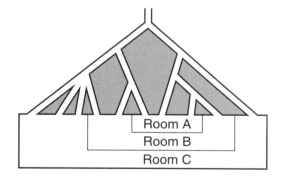

   a. About how many people would you expect to end up in Room A? _____

   b. About how many people would you expect to end up in Room B? _____

   c. About how many people would you expect to end up in Room C? _____

A Random Draw

Boxes 1, 2, and 3 contain letter tiles as shown below.

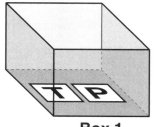
Box 1

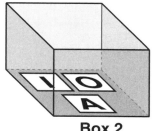
Box 2

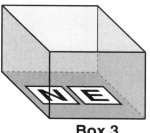
Box 3

SRB
143 144

Suppose that, without looking, you draw one letter from each box. You lay the letters in a row—the Box-1 letter first, the Box-2 letter second, and the Box-3 letter third. Then you look to see whether you have formed a word.

Example

If you draw the letter *P* from Box 1, *A* from Box 2, and *E* from Box 3, you get PAE. "PAE" is not a word in the English language.

1. List all possible letter-tile combinations.

_____

_____

_____

_____

2. What is the probability that the three letters you draw will form an English word? The word may not be an abbreviation or a person's name.

_____

3. Explain how you found your answer.

_____

_____

_____

_____

_____

_____

Venn Diagrams

There are 200 girls at Washington Middle School.
- 30 girls are on the track team.
- 38 girls are on the basketball team.
- 8 girls are on both the track team and the basketball team.

1. Fill in and label this Venn diagram to show the number of girls on each of the two teams.

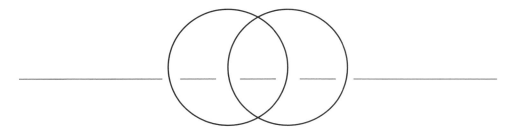

2. How many girls are on at least one of these two teams? _____ girls

3. How many girls are on the track team but not the basketball team? _____ girls

4. How many girls are on the basketball team but not the track team? _____ girls

5. How many girls are on one of these teams but not both? _____ girls

6. What percent of all the girls in the school are on at least one of these two teams? _____

7. What percent of the girls are on the track team but not the basketball team? _____

8. What percent of the girls are on the basketball team but not the track team? _____

9. What percent of the girls are on both the track team and the basketball team? _____

10. What percent of the girls are on neither the track team nor the basketball team? _____

Games of Chance

1. Design a spinner for each of the statements below.
   Use black and white sections in your designs.

   SRB 142

   a. There is about a 45% chance that the spinner will land on white.

   b. There is a little less than a 25% chance that the spinner will land on black.
   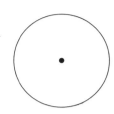

   c. The probability that the spinner will land on white is $\frac{1}{3}$.

   d. It is not likely that the spinner will land on white.

   e. The spinner will land on white $\frac{4}{5}$ of the time.

   f. The spinner will land on black about 3 times as often as it will land on white.

   g. The probability of the spinner landing on black is 5%.

2. Is it possible to play a fair game with any of the spinners above? _____

   Explain.

   _____

   _____

Reviewing Probability

1. Each fraction in the left column below shows the probability of a chance event. Match each fraction with the correct description.

$\frac{1}{3}$ The probability of getting HEADS if you flip a coin.

$\frac{1}{4}$ The probability that 3 will come up if you roll a 6-sided die.

$\frac{1}{2}$ The probability of choosing a red ball from a bag containing 2 red balls, 3 white balls, and 1 green ball.

$\frac{1}{6}$ The probability of drawing a heart from a deck of playing cards.

2. Sandy is planning her outfit for the school dance. She has narrowed her choices to a red, white, or blue dress and to a pair of red or white shoes. Make a tree diagram to show all possible combinations of dresses and shoes.

3. How many different combinations are there? _____

4. If Sandy chooses her outfit at random, what is the probability that she will choose a dress and shoes of the same color? _____

5. Ten of the students in Mrs. Moore's class play the piano. Two of the 10 also play the guitar. In all, 15 students play the piano, the guitar, or both the piano and guitar. Use this information to complete the Venn diagram at the right.

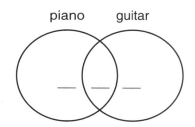

piano   guitar

6. How many students play the guitar but not the piano? _____

7. There are 25 students in Mrs. Moore's class. If you choose a student's name at random, what is the probability that the student plays the piano, the guitar, or both the piano and the guitar? _____

Family Letter

Unit 8: Rates and Ratios

The next unit is devoted to the study of rates and ratios. Both fraction and decimal notation will be used to express rates and ratios and to solve problems.

Ratios compare quantities that have the same unit. These units "cancel" each other in the comparison, so the resulting ratio has no units. For example, the fraction $\frac{2}{20}$ could mean that 2 out of 20 people in a class got an A on a test or that 20,000 out of 200,000 people voted for a certain candidate in an election.

Another frequent use of ratios is to indicate relative size. For example, a picture in a dictionary drawn to $\frac{1}{10}$ scale means that every length in the picture is $\frac{1}{10}$ the corresponding length in the actual object. Students will use ratios to characterize relative size as they examine map scales and compare geometric figures.

Rates, on the other hand, compare quantities that have different units. For example, rate of travel, or speed, may be expressed in miles per hour (55 mph); food costs may be expressed in cents per ounce (17 cents per ounce) or dollars per pound ($2.49 per pound).

Easy ratio and rate problems can be solved intuitively by making tables, similar to "What's My Rule?" tables. Problems requiring more complicated calculations are best solved by writing and solving proportions. Students will learn to solve proportions by cross multiplication. This method is based on the idea that two fractions are equivalent, if the product of the denominator of the first fraction and the numerator of the second fraction is equal to the product of the numerator of the first fraction and the denominator of the second fraction. For example, the fractions $\frac{4}{6}$ and $\frac{6}{9}$ are equivalent because $6 * 6 = 4 * 9$. This method is especially powerful because proportions can be used to solve any ratio and rate problem. It will be used extensively in algebra and trigonometry.

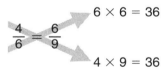

$$6 \times 6 = 36$$
$$\frac{4}{6} = \frac{6}{9}$$
$$4 \times 9 = 36$$

Students will apply these rate and ratio skills as they explore nutrition guidelines. The class will collect nutrition labels and design balanced meals based on recommended daily allowances of fat, protein, and carbohydrate. You may wish to participate by planning a balanced dinner together and by examining food labels while shopping with your child. Your child will also collect and tabulate various kinds of information about your family and your home and then compare the data by converting them to ratios. In a final application lesson, your child will learn about the Golden Ratio—a ratio that is found in many works of art and architecture.

Vocabulary

Important terms in Unit 8:

Golden Ratio A ratio of approximately 1.618 to 1. The Golden Ratio is sometimes denoted by the Greek letter φ.

n-to-1 ratio A ratio of a number to 1. Every ratio can be converted to an *n*-to-1 ratio. For example, to convert the ratio of 3 girls to 2 boys to an *n*-to-1 ratio, divide 3 by 2. The *n*-to-1 ratio is 1.5 to 1.

part-to-part ratio A ratio that compares a part of a whole to another part of the same whole. For example, the statement "There are 8 boys for every 12 girls" expresses a part-to-part ratio.

part-to-whole ratio A ratio that compares a part of a whole to the whole. For example, the statements "8 out of 20 students are boys" and "12 out of 20 students are girls" both express part-to-whole ratios.

per-unit rate A rate with 1 in the denominator.

proportion A number model that states that two fractions are equal. Often the fractions in a proportion represent rates or ratios. For example, the problem "Alan's speed is 12 miles per hour. At the same speed, how far can he travel in 3 hours?" can be modeled by the proportion $\frac{12 \text{ miles}}{1 \text{ hour}} = \frac{n \text{ miles}}{3 \text{ hours}}$.

rate A comparison by division of two quantities with unlike units. For example, a speed such as 55 miles per hour is a rate that compares distance to time.

ratio A comparison by division of two quantities with like units. Ratios can be expressed as fractions, decimals, percents, or words. Sometimes they are written with a colon between the two numbers being compared. For example, if a team wins 3 games out of 5 games played, the ratio of wins to total games can be written as $\frac{3}{5}$, 3 / 5, 0.6, 60%, 3 to 5, or 3:5 (read "three to five").

size-change factor A number that indicates the amount of an enlargement or reduction.

Do-Anytime Activities

To work with your child on the concepts taught in this unit and in previous units, try these interesting and rewarding activities:

1 Look with your child through newspapers and magazines for photos and check them to see if a size-change factor is mentioned in the caption: that is, 2X for an enlarged photo 2 times life-size; or $\frac{1}{2}$X for a photo reduced by half. You might find photos of insects, stars, bacteria, and so on. Have your child explain to you what the size-change factor means.

2 Encourage your child to read nutrition labels. Have him or her calculate the percent of fat in the item.

$$\frac{\text{fat calories}}{\text{total calories}} = \frac{?}{100} = ?\% \text{ of fat}$$

Your child should use cross multiplication to solve the problem. If he or she enjoys this activity, extend it by figuring the percent of protein and carbohydrate.

3 Help your child distinguish between part-to-part and part-to-whole ratios. When comparing a favorite team's record, decide which ratio is being used. For example, wins to losses (such as 5 to 15) or losses to wins (15 to 5) are part-to-part ratios. Part-to-whole ratios are used to compare wins to all games played (5 out of 20) or losses to all games played (15 out of 20).

Use with Lesson 7.9.

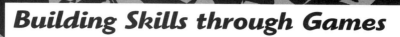

Building Skills through Games

In this unit, your child will develop his or her understanding of equivalent expressions by playing the following game. For detailed instructions, see the *Student Reference Book.*

Spoon Scramble See *Student Reference Book,* page 305
Playing *Spoon Scramble* helps students practice finding fraction, decimal, and percent parts of a whole. Four players need a deck of 16 *Spoon Scramble* cards to play this game.

As You Help Your Child with Homework

As your child brings assignments home, you may want to go over the instructions together, clarifying them as necessary. The answers listed below will guide you through some of the Study Links in this unit.

Study Link 8.1

2. a.

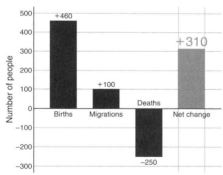

Changes in the U.S. Population, Per Hour

b. Births: +11,040 per day; +4,029,600 per year
Migrations: +2,400 per day; +876,000 per year
Deaths: −6,000 per day; −2,190,000 per year
Net Change: +310 per hour; +7,440 per day; +2,715,600 per year

3. increases; 5

Study Link 8.2

1. 3 * 12 = 36; 36 pencils

2. 36 ÷ 3 = 12; 12 friends

3. 36 ÷ 12 = 3; 3 pencils

4. Sample answers: Miles per gallon; yards per carry (in football); dollars per pound; calories per serving; paper clips per box; cookies per box

5. $8.00 per hour; $280 per week

6. 168 miles

7. The 24-oz box; $\frac{\$1.49}{20 \text{ oz}}$ = $0.0745 per ounce; $\frac{\$1.72}{24 \text{ oz}}$ = $0.0717 per ounce. The 24-oz box costs slightly less per ounce.

8.

Time (hr) (h)	Earnings ($) (8 * h)
1	8
2	16
3	24
5	40
7	56

Andy would earn $44.

Study Link 8.3

1. a. $0.13 per worm **b.** $3.38

2. a. $0.18 per ounce **b.** $2.88

3. 150,000 people **4.** 625 gallons

5. $39; $702 **6.** $\frac{1}{2}$ cent

7. 16 hours; Sample answer: 128 oz = 1 gal; 12 gal = 1,536 oz; 1,536 oz / 1.6 oz per min = 960 min; 960 min / 60 min per hour = 16 hr

Use with Lesson 7.9.

Study Link 8.4

Answers vary.

Study Link 8.5

Sample answers:

1. Corn flakes, butter, skim milk, blueberry muffin, orange juice

2.

Food	Total Calories	Calories from Fat
Corn flakes	95	trace
Butter	25	25
Skim milk	85	0
Blueberry muffin	110	30
Orange juice	110	0
Total	425	55

3. About 13%

Study Link 8.6

1. 25

2. 27

3. 24; 40

4. San Miguel Middle School; Sample answer: I wrote a ratio comparing the number of students to the number of teachers for each school. Then I reduced each ratio to its simplest form. Richards Middle School has a ratio of $\frac{14}{1}$; San Miguel, $\frac{13}{1}$.

5. Shelf 3: 8; 20; 36   Shelf 6: 14; 35; 63

6. 8; 28

Study Link 8.7

1. 20%   **2.** 64   **3.** 27

5. a. About 125   **b.** About 62.5

6. a. About 200   **b.** About 2

Study Link 8.8

Answers vary for Problems 1–4.

5. a. $6\frac{1}{2}$ in.; $4\frac{3}{4}$ in.   **b.** 5 in.; 3 in.

     c. $7\frac{1}{4}$ in.; $3\frac{3}{4}$ in.   **d.** $9\frac{1}{2}$ in.; $4\frac{1}{4}$ in.

     e. 11 in.; $8\frac{1}{2}$ in.

6. Answers vary.

7. a. $6\frac{1}{2}$ **b.** 11

Study Link 8.9

1. a. 6.4 cm   **b.** 3.2 cm

2. a. 4.5 cm   **b.** 18 cm

3. a. 4.5 cm   **b.** 1.5 cm

4. a. 5.5 cm   **b.** 16.5 cm

Study Link 8.10

2. yes; Sample answer: The perimeter of the smaller triangle, 18, is $\frac{1}{2}$ the perimeter of the larger, 36. The ratio 1 to 2 is the same as that for the sides of the similar triangles.

Study Link 8.11

1. 1.2

2. 1.65; no; Sample answer: The ratio for a standard sheet of paper is about 1.3 to 1.

3. Lucille; Sample answer: Compare ratios of problems correct to problems. Jeffrey's ratio is 0.93 to 1; Lucille's ratio is 0.94 to 1.

4. 12

5. 2.8

Study Link 8.12

1. a. 3.14 to 1   **b.** 1.6 to 1

     c. 2 to 1   **d.** 1 to 1

     e. 3 to 5

2. a. 40%   **b.** 3:5, or $\frac{3}{5}$

3. b. $7.50   **c.** 8 cans

4. a. 24 members   **b.** $\frac{3}{5} = \frac{12}{n}$; 20 free throws

Population Calculations

1. Bring nutrition labels from a variety of food packages and cans to class. A sample label is shown at the right.

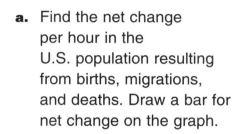

Nutrition Facts
Serving Size 1 slice (23 g)
Servings Per Container 20

Amount Per Serving

Calories 65   Calories from Fat 9

% Daily Value

Total Fat 1 g   **2%**

Total Carbohydrate 12 g   **4%**

Protein 2 g

2. The U.S. population is changing continually because of births, migrations, and deaths. The bar graph below shows U.S. population changes per hour.

   a. Find the net change per hour in the U.S. population resulting from births, migrations, and deaths. Draw a bar for net change on the graph.

   b. Find the changes per day and per year. Record them in the table below.

Changes in the U.S. Population, per Hour

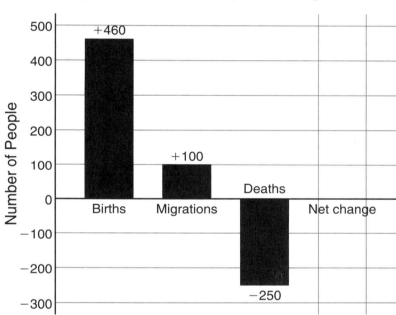

Changes in the U.S. Population

Type of Change	Per Hour	Per Day	Per Year
Births	+460		
Migrations	+100		
Deaths	−250		
Net Change			

3. Estimate the net change per minute.

   The U.S. population _____ by about _____ people per minute.
   increases/decreases

Blast from the Past

Third Grade

1. Robert has 3 packages of pencils. There are 12 pencils in each package. How many pencils does he have in all?

Number model _____

Answer _____
(unit)

units	packages	pencils per packages	pencils
numbers			

2. Robert gives 3 pencils to each of his friends. How many friends can get 3 pencils each?

Number model _____

Answer _____
(unit)

units	friends	pencils per friends	pencils
numbers			

3. What if Robert shares his pencils equally between himself and 11 friends? How many pencils does each person get?

Number model _____

Answer _____
(unit)

units	friends	pencils per friends	pencils
numbers			

Fourth Grade

4. Give 6 examples of rates.

a. _____   **b.** _____

c. _____   **d.** _____

e. _____   **f.** _____

5. Tina works 7 hours a day, 5 days a week. She earns $56 per day.

a. How much does she earn per hour? _____

b. How much does she earn per week? _____

6. The Davis family drove 280 miles to visit relatives. It took 5 hours. At that rate, how many miles did the family drive in 3 hours? _____

Fill in the rate table, if needed.

hours						
miles						

7. A store charges $1.49 for a 20-ounce box of Puff Flakes cereal and $1.72 for a 24-ounce box of the same cereal. Which is the better buy? _____

Explain. _____

_____

_____

Fifth Grade

8. Complete the table below. Then graph the data. Connect the points.

Andy earns $8 per hour. *Rule:* Earnings = $8 ∗ number of hours worked

Time (hr) (h)	Earnings ($) ($8 * h$)
1	
2	
3	
	40
7	

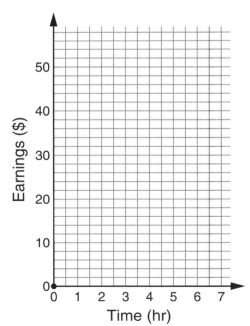

Earnings ($) vs Time (hr)

Plot a point to show Andy's earnings for $5\frac{1}{2}$ hours.
How much will he earn? _____

Calculating Rates

If necessary, draw a picture, find a per-unit rate, make a rate table, or use a proportion to help you solve these problems.

1. A can of worms for fishing costs $2.60. There are 20 worms in a can.

    a. What is the cost per worm? _____

    b. At this rate, how much would 26 worms cost? _____

2. An 11-ounce bag of chips costs $1.99.

    a. What is the cost per ounce,
    rounded to the nearest cent? _____

    b. What is the cost per pound, rounded to the nearest cent? _____

3. Just 1 gram of venom from a king cobra snake can kill 150 people. At this rate, about how many people would 1 kilogram kill? _____

4. A good milking cow produces nearly 6,000 quarts of milk each year. At this rate, about how many gallons of milk will a cow produce in 5 months? _____

5. A dog-walking service costs $117 for 6 months.

    What is the cost for 2 months? _____ For 3 years? _____

Challenge

6. A 1-pound bag of candy, containing 502 pieces, costs 16.8 cents per ounce. What is the cost of 1 piece of candy? Circle the best answer.

      1.86 cents   2.99 cents   0.33 cent $\frac{1}{2}$ cent

7. Mr. Rainier's car uses about 1.6 fluid ounces of gas per minute when the engine is idling. One night, he parked his car but forgot to turn off the motor. He had just filled his tank. His tank holds 12 gallons.

    About how many hours will it take before his car runs out of gas? _____

    Explain what you did to find the answer. _____

    _____

    _____

Sources: 2201 Fascinating Facts; Everything Has Its Price

Food Costs as Unit Rates

Visit a grocery store in the next day or two. Select 10 different items and record the cost and weight of each item in the table below.

- Select items that include a wide range of weights—from very light to very heavy.

- Select only items whose containers list weights in pounds, ounces, or a combination of pounds and ounces (such as 2 lb 6 oz).

- Do not choose produce items (fruits and vegetables).

- Do not choose milk, ice cream, soft drinks, juices, or other liquid items. Liquid items are usually sold by volume, not by weight. Their containers list volumes (gallons, quarts, liters, or fluid ounces).

Item	Cost	Weight Shown	Weight in Ounces	Cents per Ounce	Weight in Pounds	Dollars per Pound

1. Convert each weight to ounces. Calculate the unit cost in cents per ounce.

2. Convert each weight to pounds. Calculate the unit cost in dollars per pound.

Example A jar of pickles weighs 1 lb 5 oz and costs $2.39.	
Convert weight	**Calculate cost**
to ounces: 1 lb 5 oz = 21 oz	in cents per ounce: $\frac{\$2.39}{21 \text{ oz}} = \frac{11.4 \text{ cents}}{1 \text{ oz}}$
to pounds: 1 lb 5 oz = $1\frac{5}{16}$ lb = 1.31 lb	in dollars per pound: $\frac{\$2.39}{1.31 \text{ lb}} = \frac{\$1.82}{1 \text{ lb}}$

Calculating Calories from Fat

Study Link
8.5

1. Choose 5 items from the following menu that you would like to have for breakfast. Choose your favorite foods. Pay no attention to total calories, but try to limit the percent of calories from fat to 30% or less. Put a check mark next to each item.

Food	Total Calories	Calories from Fat
Toast (1 slice)	70	10
Corn flakes (8 oz)	95	trace
Oatmeal (8 oz)	130	20
Butter (1 pat)	25	25
Doughnut	205	105
Jam (1 tbs)	55	trace
Pancakes (butter, syrup)	180	60
Bacon (2 slices)	85	65
Yogurt	240	25
Sugar (1 tsp)	15	0
Scrambled eggs (2)	140	90
Fried eggs (2)	175	125
Hash browns	130	65
Skim milk (8 fl oz)	85	0
2% milk (8 fl oz)	145	45
Blueberry muffin	110	30
Orange juice (8 fl oz)	110	0
Bagel	165	20
Bagel with cream cheese	265	105

2. Record the 5 items you chose in the table. Fill in the rest of the table, and then find the total number of calories for each column.

Food	Total Calories	Calories from Fat
Total		

3. What percent of the total number of calories comes from fat? _____

Solving Ratio Problems

**Study Link
8.6**

Solve the following problems. Use coins or two-color counters to help you. If you need to draw pictures, use the back of this page.

SRB
116–118

1. You have 45 coins. Five out of every 9 are HEADS up and the rest are TAILS up. How many coins are HEADS up? _____ coins

2. You have 36 coins. The ratio of HEADS-up coins to TAILS-up coins is 3 to 1. How many coins are HEADS up? _____ coins

3. You have 16 coins that are HEADS up and 18 coins that are TAILS up. After you add some coins that are TAILS up, the ratio of HEADS-up coins to TAILS-up coins is 1 to 1.5.

   How many coins are TAILS up? _____ coins   How many coins in all? _____ coins

4. At Richards Middle School, there are 448 students and 32 teachers. The San Miguel Middle School has 234 students and 18 teachers. Which school has a better ratio of students to teachers, that is, fewer students per teacher? _____

   Explain how you found your answer. _____

   _____

   _____

   _____

5. There are six shelves for books. Numbers of books are listed in the table. The ratio of mystery books to adventure books to humor books is the same on each shelf. Complete the table.

Shelf	Mystery Books	Adventure Books	Humor Books
1	4	10	18
2	6		
3			
4		25	
5	12		
6			63

Challenge

6. You have a number of coins. The ratio of HEADS-up coins to TAILS-up coins is 2 to 5. Fewer than 10 coins are HEADS up, and more than 15 coins are TAILS up.

   a. How many coins are HEADS up? _____ coins

   b. How many coins are there in all? _____ coins

Body Composition by Weight

Solve.

1. About 1 out of every 5 pounds of the body weight of an average adult is fat. What percent of body weight is fat? _____

2. Muscles make up about 40% of the body weight of an average adult. About how many pounds do the muscles of a 160-pound adult weigh? _____ lb

3. About 18% of the total body weight of an adult is bone. The rest is mostly water and other fluids. If an adult weighs 150 pounds, about how many pounds are bone? _____ lb

4. The human body contains a number of different elements. The table gives the percents of various elements in the human body. Fill in the missing number in the table.

Use the information in the table to set up proportions and solve the following problems.

Element	%
Carbon	50%
Oxygen	20%
Hydrogen	10%
Nitrogen	8.5%
Calcium	4%
Phosphorus	2.5%
Potassium	1%
Other	

5. a. If the weight of all of the oxygen in an adult's body is about 25 pounds, what is the total weight of this adult? About _____ lb

   b. What is the approximate weight of the carbon in that adult's body? About _____ lb

6. a. If the weight of the calcium in an adult's body is about 8 pounds, what is the total weight of this adult? About _____ lb

   b. What is the approximate weight of the potassium? About _____ lb

Source: Numbers: How Many, How Far, How Long, How Much

Home Data

1. Record the following data about all of the members of your household.

   a. Total number of people _____ b. Number of males _____

   c. Number of females _____ d. Number of left-handed people _____

   e. Number of right-handed people _____ (For people who are ambidextrous, record the hand most often used for writing.)

For the rectangles in this Study Link, use length as the measure of the longer sides and width as the measure of the shorter sides.

2. Find an American flag or a picture of one. Measure its length and width.

   a. length _____
      (unit)

   b. width _____
      (unit)

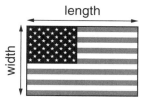

3. Measure the length and width of a television screen to the nearest $\frac{1}{2}$ inch.

   a. length _____
      (unit)

   b. width _____
      (unit)

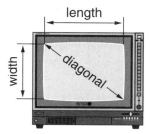

4. Find three books of different sizes, such as a small paperback, your journal, and a large reference book. Measure the length and width of each book to the nearest $\frac{1}{2}$ inch.

 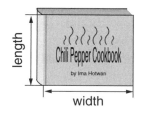 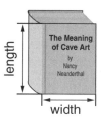

   a. Small book: length _____ width _____
                            (unit)   (unit)

   b. Medium book: length _____ width _____
                            (unit)   (unit)

   c. Large book: length _____ width _____
                            (unit)   (unit)

5. Find samples of the following items. Measure the length and width of each to the nearest $\frac{1}{4}$ inch.

a. Postcard length _____ (unit) width _____ (unit)

b. Index card length _____ (unit) width _____ (unit)

c. Envelope (regular) length _____ (unit) width _____ (unit)

d. Envelope (business) length _____ (unit) width _____ (unit)

e. Notebook paper length _____ (unit) width _____ (unit)

6. Show the four rectangles below to each member of your household. Ask each person to select the rectangle that he or she "likes best" or "thinks is the nicest looking." Tally the answers. Remember to include your own choice.

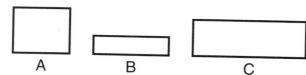

A   B   C   D

Voting Results	A	B	C	D
Tally of Votes				
Number of Votes				

7. Measure the "rise" and "run" of stairs in your home. The diagram shows what these dimensions are. (If there are no stairs in your home, measure stairs outdoors or in a friend's or neighbor's home.)

a. rise _____ in.   **b.** run _____ in.

Scale Drawings

 Study Link
8.9

Measure the object in each drawing to the nearest millimeter. Then use the size-change factor to determine the actual size of the object.

Size-change Factor: $\dfrac{\text{changed length}}{\text{original length}}$

1. a. diameter in drawing: _____

    b. actual diameter: _____

Size-change	Size-change Factor
Scale 2:1	

2. a. height in drawing:

    _____

    b. actual height:

    _____

CRAFT GLUE

Size-change	Size-change Factor
$\frac{1}{4}$X	

3. a. length in drawing:

    _____

    b. actual length:

    _____

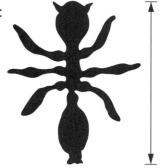

Size-change	Size-change Factor
Scale 3:1	

4. a. height in drawing: _____

    b. actual length: _____

Size-change	Size-change Factor
Scale 1:3	

Similar Polygons

1. Find the missing lengths of sides for these pairs of similar polygons.

SRB
167

a.

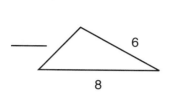
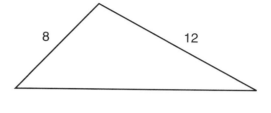

b.

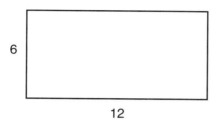

c.

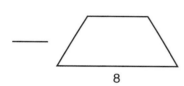
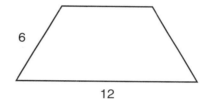

d.

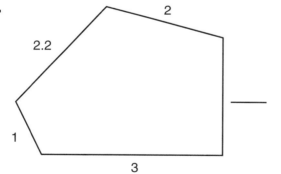
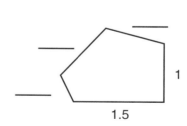

2. You know that a size-change factor expresses a ratio for lengths only—not for angles, areas, or volumes. Do you think that a size-change factor also applies to perimeters of similar polygons? _____

   Use the pairs of similar polygons in Problem 1 to defend your answer.

   _____

   _____

   _____

Comparing Ratios

1. A dictionary measures 24 centimeters by 20 centimeters.

   The ratio of its length to its width is about _____ to 1.

   Explain how you found your answer.

   _____

   _____

2. A sheet of legal-sized paper measures 14 inches by
   $8\frac{1}{2}$ inches. The ratio of its length to its width is about _____ to 1.

   Is this the same ratio as for a sheet of
   paper that measures 11 inches by $8\frac{1}{2}$ inches? _____

   Explain.

   _____

   _____

3. Jeffrey got 28 out of 30 problems correct on his math test. Lucille got 47
   out of 50 problems correct on her math test. Who did better on the test? _____

   Explain.

   _____

   _____

4. A ruler is 30 centimeters long and 2.5 centimeters
   wide. The ratio of its length to its width is about _____ to 1.

Challenge

5. If a ruler is 33.6 centimeters long, about how
   wide would it have to be to have the same ratio
   of length to width as the ruler in Problem 4?   _____ centimeters

   Explain how you found your answer.

   _____

   _____

Rate and Ratio Review

1. Match each ratio on the left with one of the ratios on the right.

   a. Circumference to diameter of a circle   _____   1.6 to 1

   b. Length to width of a Golden Rectangle   _____   3 to 5

   c. Diameter to radius of a circle   _____   2 to 1

   d. Length of one side of a square to another   _____   3.14 to 1

   e. 12 correct answers out of 20 problems   _____   1 to 1

2. Refer to the following numbers to answer the questions below.

   1   2   3   4   5   6   7   8   9   10

   a. What percent of the numbers are prime numbers? _____

   b. What is the ratio of the numbers
   divisible by 3 to the numbers divisible by 2? _____

3. A 12-pack of Chummy Cola costs $3 at Stellar Supermart.

   a. Complete the rate table below to find the per-unit rates.

dollars		3.00	1.00
cans	1	12	

   b. At this price, how much would 30 cans of Chummy Cola cost? _____

   c. How many cans could you buy for $2.00? _____

4. Complete or write a proportion for each problem. Then solve the problem.

   a. Only $\frac{4}{9}$ of the club members voted in the last election. There are
   54 members in the club. How many members voted?

   Proportion $\frac{4}{9} = \frac{x}{54}$ Answer _____

   b. During basketball practice, Christina made 3 out of every 5 free throws
   she attempted. If she made 12 free throws, how many free throws did she
   attempt in all?

   Proportion _____   Answer _____

Rate and Ratio Review (cont.)

5. a. Draw circles and squares so that the ratio of circles to squares is 3 to 2 and the total number of shapes is 10.

b. Draw circles and squares so that the ratio of circles to total shapes is 2 to 3 and the total number of squares is 2.

c. Draw circles and squares so that the ratio of circles to squares is 1 to 3 and the total number of shapes is 12.

6. The city is planning to build a new park. The park will be rectangular in shape, approximately 800 feet long and 625 feet wide. Make a scale drawing of the park on the $\frac{1}{2}$-inch grid paper below.

Scale: $\frac{1}{2}$ inch represents 100 feet

Use with Lesson 8.12.

Unit 9: More about Variables, Formulas, and Graphs

You may be surprised at some of the topics that are covered in Unit 9. Several of them would be traditionally introduced in a first-year algebra course. If you are assisting your child, you might find it useful to refer to the *Student Reference Book* to refresh your memory about topics you have not studied for a number of years.

Your child has been applying many mathematical properties, starting as early as first grade. In Unit 9, the class will explore and apply one of these properties, the distributive property, which can be stated as follows:

For any numbers a, b, and c, $a * (b + c) = (a * b) + (a * c)$.

Students will use this property to simplify algebraic expressions. They will use these simplification procedures, together with the equation-solving methods that were presented in Unit 6, to solve more difficult equations that contain parentheses or like terms on at least one side of the equal sign. Here is an example:

To solve the equation $5(b + 3) - 3b + 5 = 4(b - 1)$,

1. Use the distributive property
   to remove the parentheses. $5b + 15 - 3b + 5 = 4b - 4$

2. Combine like terms. $2b + 20 = 4b - 4$

3. Solve the equation. $20 = 2b - 4$

                                                   $24 = 2b$

                                                   $b = 12$

Much of Unit 9 also focuses on applying formulas—in computer spreadsheets and in calculating the areas of circles, rectangles, triangles, and parallelograms, the perimeters of polygons, and the circumferences of circles. Formulas for calculating the volumes of rectangular prisms, cylinders, and spheres will also be used to solve a variety of interesting problems.

Finally, your child will be introduced to the Pythagorean Theorem, which states that if a and b are the lengths of the legs of a right triangle and c is the length of the hypotenuse, then $a^2 + b^2 = c^2$. By applying this theorem, students will learn how to calculate long distances indirectly—that is, without actually measuring them.

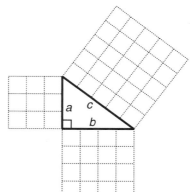

Please keep this Family Letter for reference as your child works through Unit 9.

Vocabulary

Important terms in Unit 9:

distributive property A property that relates multiplication and addition or subtraction. This property gets its name because it "distributes" a factor over terms inside parentheses.

equivalent equations Equations that have the same solution. For example, $2 + x = 4$ and $6 + x = 8$ are equivalent equations because the solution to both is $x = 2$.

hypotenuse In a right triangle, the side opposite the right angle.

indirect measurement Method for determining heights, distances, and other quantities that cannot be measured directly.

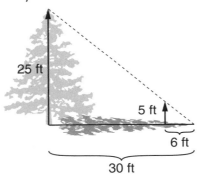

leg of a right triangle A side of a right triangle that is not the *hypotenuse*.

like terms In an algebraic expression, either the constant terms or any terms that contain the same variable(s) raised to the same power(s). For example, $4y$ and $7y$ are like terms in the expression $4y + 7y - z$.

Pythagorean Theorem The following famous theorem: If the *legs of a right triangle* have lengths a and b and the hypotenuse has length c, then $a^2 + b^2 = c^2$.

simplify an expression or an equation To rewrite an equation or an expression by removing parentheses and combining like terms and constants. For example, $7y + 4 + 5 + 3y$ can be simplified as $10y + 9$; and $2(a + 4) = 4a + 1 + 3$ can be simplified as $2a + 8 = 4a + 4$.

trial-and-error method A method for finding the solution of an equation by trying several test numbers.

Use with Lesson 8.13.

Do-Anytime Activities

To work with your child on the concepts taught in this unit and previous units, try these interesting and rewarding activities:

1 To practice simplifying expressions and solving equations, ask your child to bring home the game materials for *Algebra Election*. Game directions are in the *Student Reference Book*.

2 If other children in your home have mobiles in their rooms, ask your sixth grader to explain to you how to balance it perfectly. Have your child show you the equations he or she used to balance it.

3 Your child may need extra practice with the partial-quotients division algorithm. Have him or her show you this method. Provide a few problems to practice at home, and have your child explain the steps to you as he or she works through them.

As You Help Your Child with Homework

As your child brings assignments home, you may want to go over the instructions together, clarifying them as necessary. The answers listed below will guide you through this unit's Study Links.

Study Link 9.1

1. a. $(8 * 4) + (7 * 4)$ b. $(8 * 6) + (5 * 6)$
   $4 * (7 + 8)$ $6 * (5 + 8)$
                       $(8 + 5) * 6$
   c. $(4 + 9) * 3$
   $(9 * 3) + (4 * 3)$
2. a. 6
   b. $\underline{(9 - 3)} * \underline{5} = \underline{30}; \underline{(9 * 5)} - \underline{(3 * 5)} = \underline{30}$
3. a. N   b. O
   c. O   d. N
   e. P   f. O
4. \$3.52 $(8 * 0.10) + (8 * 0.34) = 3.52$

Study Link 9.2

1. a. $(7 * 3) + (7 * 4)$
   b. $(7 * 3) + (7 * \pi)$
   c. $(7 * 3) + (7 * y)$
   d. $(7 * 3) + (7 * (2 * 4))$
   e. $(7 * 3) + (7 * (2 * \pi))$
   f. $(7 * 3) + (7 * (2 * y))$

2. b. $(20 * 42) - (20 * 19) = 840 - 380 = 460$
   c. $(32 * 40) + (50 * 40) = 1,280 + 2,000 = 3,280$
   d. $(90 * 11) - (8 * 11) = 990 - 88 = 902$
   e. $(9 * 15) + (9 * 25) = 135 + 225 = 360$
3. a. $(80 * 5) + (120 * 5) = (80 + 120) * 5$
   c. $12(d - t) = 12d - 12t$
   d. $(a + c) * n = a * n + c * n$
   f. $(9 * \frac{1}{2}) - (\frac{1}{3} * \frac{1}{2}) = (9 - \frac{1}{3}) * \frac{1}{2}$

Study Link 9.3

1. $15x$ 2. $\frac{3}{10}y$ 3. $-11t$
4. d 5. -6 6. $3p$
7. -3 8. 8.3 9. $7b + 14$
10. $1\frac{1}{6}a + \frac{1}{4}t$

Study Link 9.4

1. $-y + 2b + 24$ 2. $64 + 32k$ 3. $12s$

Use with Lesson 8.13.

203

Study Link 9.5

Column 1	Column 2
A $\quad 4x - 2 = 6$	$\underline{C}$ $\quad 6j + 8 = 8 + 6j$
Solution: $x = 2$	$\underline{A}$ $\quad 2c - 1 = 3$

Study Link 0·0

1. 11　　　　2. 4

	$\underline{B}$ $\quad 6w = -12$
	$\underline{C}$ $\quad \frac{2h}{2h} = 3.17$
	$\underline{A}$ $\quad \frac{3q}{3} - 6 = -4$
	$\underline{A}$ $\quad 3(r + 4) = 18$
B $\quad 3s = -6$	$\underline{C}$ $\quad 2(5x + 1) = 10x + 2$
Solution: $s = -2$	$\underline{A}$ $\quad -5x - 5(2 - x) = 2(x - 7)$
	$\underline{D}$ $\quad s = 0$
	$\underline{B}$ $\quad 5b - 3 - 2b = 6b + 3$
C $\quad 3y - 2y = y$	$\underline{B}$ $\quad \frac{t}{4} + 3 = 2\frac{1}{2}$
Solution: $y =$ any	$\underline{A}$ $\quad 6z = 12$
number	$\underline{D}$ $\quad 2a = (4 + 7)a$

D $\quad 5a = 7a$

Solution: $a = 0$

Study Link 9.6

1. 7　　　　2. 38　　　　3. 4

4. 2　　　　5. $23 + 14y$　　　6. $-2b + 32$

7. $3f - 55 - 10e$

8. $225 + 35g$

9. $r + 23$

10. $4b + 72; 72 - (-4b)$

11. $W = 5b; D = 4; w = 30; d = 12$
Equation: $5b * 4 = 30 * 12$; Solution: $b = 18$
Weight of the object on the left: 90 units

Study Link 9.7

3. About 2.7 feet

Study Link 9.8

1. 112 in.^{2}　　2. 2.5 ft^2　　3. 108 cm^2

4. 45.5 mm^2　　5. 55 ft^2　　6. 696 m^2

7. $a * b$　　　8. $(m + n) * y$

Study Link 9.9

1. 120 in.^{3}　　2. 904.78 in.^{3}　　3. 11.97 in.^{2}

4. 10.4 m^3　　5. 3,391 yd^2　　6. 3.22 ft^3

Study Link 9.11

1. **a.** $C = \frac{5}{9} * (77 - 32)$; 25°C

　b. $50 = \frac{5}{9} * (F - 32)$; 122°F

2. **a.** $A = \frac{1}{2} * 17 * 5$; 42.5 cm^2

　b. $90 = \frac{1}{2} * 12 * h$; 15 in.

3. **a.** $V = \frac{1}{3} * \pi * 4 * 9$; 37.68 in.^{3}

　b. $94.2 = \frac{1}{3} * \pi * 9 * h$; 10 cm

Study Link 9.12

1. Sample answer: Use the Pythagorean Theorem to calculate the distance: $20^2 + 14^2 = c^2$. The distance is about 24.4 feet. The rope should be at least 29 feet long to allow for rope at each end.

2. Sample answer: It will take Jack 4 hours. Jill must travel 200 miles ($120^2 + 160^2 = 200^2$), so she should drive 50 mph to reach the meeting place in 4 hours.

3. Sample answer: $15^2 + 11^2 = 346$; $18^2 = 324$. Igor should buy a longer ladder. The distance is longer than 18 feet.

Study Link 9.13

1. **a.** $7x$　　　　　　**b.** $4x + 7$

　c. $6x + 2$　　　　**d.** 6

2. Sample answer: Cindy did not multiply 10 by 8. The simplified expression should be $(8 * x) + (8 * 10)$, or $8x + 80$.

3. **a.** $x = -10$　　　**b.** $g = -5$

　c. $y = 4$　　　　**d.** $x = 14$

4. Length of $\overline{AB}$: 5 in.; Length of $\overline{BC}$: 8 in.; Length of $\overline{AC}$: 5 in.

5. The perimeter of Right Triangle *GLD* is 12 centimeters.
Area = 6 cm^2

6. 4 blocks

Multiplying Sums

1. For each expression in the top row, find one or more equivalent expressions below it. Fill in the oval next to each equivalent expression.

a. (8 + 7) * 4

   ○ (8 * 4) + (7 * 4)

   ○ 4 * (7 + 8)

   ○ (8 + 4) * 7

   ○ (8 + 4) * (7 + 4)

b. (6 * 5) + (6 * 8)

   ○ (8 * 6) + (5 * 6)

   ○ 6 * (5 + 8)

   ○ (8 + 5) * 6

   ○ (6 + 5) * (6 + 8)

c. 3 * (9 + 4)

   ○ (9 + 4) * (3 + 4)

   ○ 9 * (3 + 4)

   ○ (4 + 9) * 3

   ○ (9 * 3) + (4 * 3)

2. The area of Rectangle M is 45 square units.

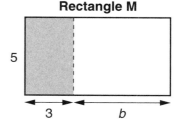

Rectangle M

   a. What is the value of *b*? _____

   b. Write two different number models to describe the area of the unshaded part of Rectangle M.

(___ − ___) * ___ = ___   (___ * ___) − (___ * ___) = ___

3. Each of the following expressions describes the area of one of the rectangles below. Write the letter of the rectangle next to the expression.

a. (3 + 2) * 7 _____

b. (2 * 3) + (7 * 3) _____

c. (7 + 2) * 3 _____

d. (3 * 7) + (2 * 7) _____

e. 2 * (7 + 3) _____

f. 3 * (2 + 7) _____

Rectangle O

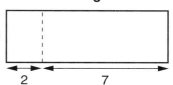

Rectangle N

Rectangle P

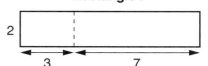

4. Marge wants to buy envelopes and stamps to send cards to eight friends. Envelopes cost $0.10 and stamps cost $0.34. How much will she spend? _____

   Write a number model to show how you solved the problem.

_____

Challenge

5. On the back of this page, explain how Problem 4 is similar to the rectangle problems.

Using the Distributive Property

> Reminder: $a * (x + y) = (a * x) + (a * y)$
> $a * (x - y) = (a * x) - (a * y)$

SRB
230 231

1. Use the distributive property to rewrite each expression.

    a. $7 * (3 + 4) = (\underline{} * \underline{}) + (\underline{} * \underline{})$

    b. $7 * (3 + \pi) = (\underline{} * \underline{}) + (\underline{} * \underline{})$

    c. $7 * (3 + y) = (\underline{} * \underline{}) + (\underline{} * \underline{})$

    d. $7 * (3 + (2 * 4)) = (\underline{} * \underline{}) + (\underline{} * (2 * 4))$

    e. $7 * (3 + (2 * \pi)) = (\underline{} * \underline{}) + (\underline{} * (2 * \underline{}))$

    f. $7 * (3 + (2 * y)) = (\underline{} * \underline{}) + (\underline{} * (\underline{} * \underline{}))$

2. Use the distributive property to solve each problem. Study the first one.

    a. $7 * (110 + 25) = $ _(7 * 110) + (7 * 25) = 770 + 175 = 945_

    b. $20 * (42 - 19) = $ _____

    c. $(32 + 50) * 40 = $ _____

    d. $(90 - 8) * 11 = $ _____

    e. $9 * (15 + 25) = $ _____

3. Circle the statements that are examples of the distributive property.

    a. $(80 * 5) + (120 * 5) = (80 + 120) * 5$

    b. $6 * (3 - 0.5) = (6 * 3) - 0.5$

    c. $12(d - t) = 12d - 12t$

    d. $(a + c) * n = a * n + c * n$

    e. $(16 + 4m) + 9.7 = 16 + (4m + 9.7)$

    f. $\left(9 * \frac{1}{2}\right) - \left(\frac{1}{3} * \frac{1}{2}\right) = \left(9 - \frac{1}{3}\right) * \frac{1}{2}$

Combining Like Terms

Simplify each expression by rewriting it as a single term.

SRB
234

1. $3x + 12x =$ _____

2. $(1\frac{3}{5})y - (1\frac{3}{10})y =$ _____

3. $-(5t) - 6t =$ _____

4. $4d + (-3d) =$ _____

Complete each equation.

5. $15k = (9 -$ _____$)k$

6. $3.6p - p =$ _____ $- 0.4p$

7. $(8 +$ _____$) * m = 5m$

8. _____ $j - 4.5j = 3.8j$

Simplify each expression by combining like terms. Check your answers by substituting the given values for the variables. Show your work.

Example $18 + 6m + 2m + 26$
           Combine the m terms. $6m + 2m = 8m$
           Combine the number terms. $18 + 26 = 44$
           So, $18 + 6m + 2m + 26 = 8m + 44$

           Check: Substitute 5 for m.
           $18 + (6 * 5) + (2 * 5) + 26 = (8 * 5) + 44$
                $18 + 30 + 10 + 26 = 40 + 44$
                          $84 = 84$

9. $8b + 9 + 4b - 3b + (-2b) - (-5) =$ _____

      Check for: $b = -6$

10. $\frac{1}{2}a + \frac{3}{4}t + \frac{2}{3}a + \left(-\frac{1}{2}t\right) =$ _____

       Check for: $a = 2$ and $t = -2$

Simplifying Expressions

Simplify each expression by removing parentheses and combining like terms.
Check by substituting the given values for the variables. Show your work.

SRB
230 231
234

1. $5(y - b) + 3b - 6y + 4(6 + b) =$ _____

Check: Substitute 1 for y and $\frac{2}{3}$ for b.

2. $(12 - 3 + 5k)6 + 4k - 2(k + 5) =$ _____

Check: Substitute 0.5 for k.

3. $3(4 + 5s) - 12 + (-3s) =$ _____

Check: Substitute $\frac{1}{3}$ for s.

Equivalent Equations

Each equation in Column 2 is equivalent to an equation in Column 1. Solve each equation in Column 1. Write "any number" if all numbers are solutions of the equation.

Match each equation in Column 1 with an equivalent equation in Column 2. Write the letter label of the equation in Column 1 next to the equivalent equation in Column 2.

Column 1	**Column 2**

A $4x - 2 = 6$

    _____ $6j + 8 = 8 + 6j$

    _____ $2c - 1 = 3$

    _____ $6w = -12$

Solution _____   _____ $\frac{2h}{2h} = 1$

B $3s = -6$ _____ $\frac{3q}{3} - 6 = -4$

    A $3(r + 4) = 18$

    _____ $2(5x + 1) = 10x + 2$

Solution _____   _____ $-5x - 5(2 - x) = 2(x - 7)$

C $3y - 2y = y$ _____ $s = 0$

    _____ $5b - 3 - 2b = 6b + 3$

    _____ $\frac{t}{4} + 3 = 2\frac{1}{2}$

Solution _____   _____ $6z = 12$

D $5a = 7a$ _____ $2a = (4 + 7)a$

Solution _____

Expressions and Equations

Solve.

           Solution   Solution

1. $3x + 9 = 30$ $x =$ _____   **2.** $73 = \frac{1}{2}(108 + e)$ $e =$ _____

3. $55 = (9 - d) * 11$ $d =$ _____   **4.** $(m * 15) + (m * 6) = 42$ $m =$ _____

Simplify these expressions by combining like terms.

5. $8y + 27 + 6y + (-4)$ _____

6. $7b + 17 - 9b + 15$ _____

7. $3f - 80 + 25 - 10e$ _____

8. $240 + 5g + 3(10g - 5)$ _____

Circle all expressions that are equivalent to the original. There may be more than one. Check your answer by substituting values for the variable.

9. Original: $3r + 17 - 2r + 6$

    $5r + 23$ $23 - r$ $r + 23$ $13 + r$

10. Original: $8(9 + b) - 4b$

    $89 - 3b$ $72 - 3b$ $4b + 72$ $72 - (-4b)$

Challenge

11. The top mobile is in balance. The fulcrum is in the center of the rod. A mobile will balance when $W * D = w * d$.

Look at the bottom mobile. What is the weight of the object on the left?

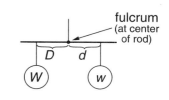

Write and solve an equation to answer the question.

    $W =$ _____ $D =$ _____ $w =$ _____ $d =$ _____

    Equation _____   Solution _____

    Weight of the object on the left _____ units

Circumferences and Areas of Circles

Circles

	A	B	C
1	circumferences and areas of circles		
2	radius (ft)	circumference (ft)	area (ft²)
3	r	$2\pi r$	πr^2
4	0.5		
5	1.0		
6	1.5	9.4	7.1
7	2.0	12.6	12.6
8	2.5		
9	3.0		

1. Complete the spreadsheet at the left. For each radius, calculate the circumference and area of the circle having that radius.

2. Use the data in the spreadsheet to graph the number pairs for radius and circumference on the first grid below. Then graph the number pairs for radius and area on the second grid below. Make line graphs by connecting the points.

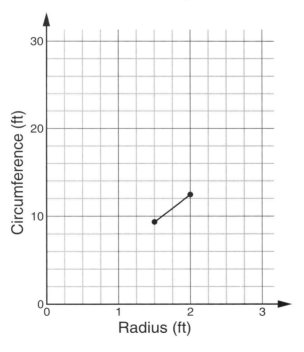

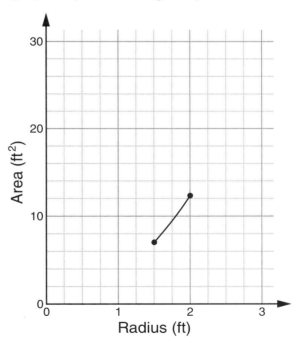

3. A circular tabletop has an area of 23 square feet. Use the second line graph to estimate the radius of the tabletop.   Radius _____ feet

Area Problems

Calculate the area of each figure in Problems 1–6. Remember to include the unit in each answer.

1. parallelogram

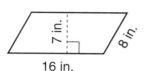

Area _____

2. rectangle

Area _____

3. parallelogram

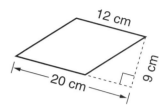

Area _____

4. triangle

Area _____

5. triangle

Area _____

6. trapezoid

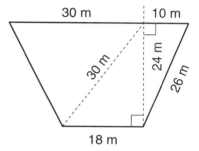

Area _____

Challenge

In Problems 7 and 8, all dimensions are given as variables. Write a true statement in terms of the variables to express the area of each figure.

Example

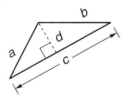

Area $\frac{1}{2} * c * d$

7.

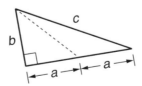

Area _____

8.

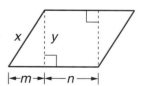

Area _____

Area and Volume Problems

Area formulas

Rectangle:	$A = b * h$
Parallelogram:	$A = b * h$
Triangle:	$A = \frac{1}{2} * b * h$

Volume formulas

Cylinder:	$V = B * h = \pi * r^2 * h$
Rectangular prism:	$V = B * h = l * w * h$
Sphere:	$V = \frac{4}{3} * \pi * r^3$

Circumference formula $C = 2\pi r$

A = area
V = volume
B = area of base
C = circumference
b = length of base
h = height
l = length
w = width
r = radius

Calculate the area or volume of each figure. Pay close attention to the units.

1.

6"
4"
5"

Volume _____

2.

diameter = 12"

Volume _____

3.

5.7"
2.1"

Area _____

4.

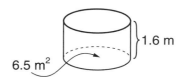

1.6 m
6.5 m²

Volume _____

5.

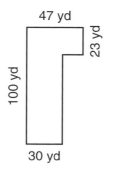

47 yd
23 yd
100 yd
30 yd

Area _____

6.

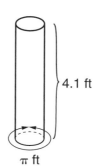

4.1 ft
π ft

Volume _____

Solving Equations by Trial and Error

SRB
223–225

Find numbers that are close to the solution of each equation.
Use the suggested test numbers to get started.

1. Equation: $r^2 + r = 15$

r	r^2	$r^2 + r$	Compare $r^2 + r$ to 15
3	9	12	< 15
4	16	20	> 15
3.5	12.25	15.75	> 15

My closest solution _____

2. Equation: $x^2 - 2x = 23$

x	x^2	$2x$	$x^2 - 2x$	Compare $x^2 - 2x$ to 23
6	36	12	24	> 23
5	25	10	15	< 23
5.5	30.25	11	19.25	< 23

My closest solution _____

Using Formulas

Each problem below states a formula and gives the values of all but one of the variables in the formula. Substitute the known values for the variables in the formula and solve the equation.

1. The formula $C = \frac{5}{9} * (F - 32)$ may be used to convert between Fahrenheit and Celsius temperatures.

    a. Convert 77°F to degrees C.

        Equation _____
        Solve.

        77°F = _____ °C

    b. Convert 50°C to degrees F.

        Equation _____
        Solve.

        50°C = _____ °F

2. The formula for the area of a trapezoid is $A = \frac{1}{2} * (a + b) * h$.

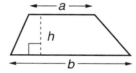

    a. Find the area (A) of a trapezoid if $a = 7$ cm, $b = 10$ cm, and $h = 5$ cm.

        Equation _____
        Solve.

        Area _____

    b. Find the height (h) of a trapezoid if $a = 6.5$ inches, $b = 5.5$ inches, and $A = 90$ inches².

        Equation _____
        Solve.

        Height _____

3. The formula for the volume of a cone is $V = \frac{1}{3} * \pi * r^2 * h$.

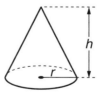

    a. Find the volume (V) of a cone if $r = 2$ inches and $h = 9$ inches.

        Equation _____
        Solve.

        Volume _____

    b. Find the height (h) of a cone if $r = 3$ cm and $V = 94.2$ cm³.

        Equation _____
        Solve.

        Height _____

Pythagoras and True Love

Pythagoras is a "Mr. Lonelyhearts" columnist for a popular newspaper. He recently received the following letters. How would you solve these lovebirds' problems?

1. Dear Pythagoras: My girlfriend Roma and I want to elope. But we have a problem. She lives in a third-floor apartment. There is a 14-foot-wide moat around the apartment, and Roma's window is 20 feet above the moat. If I throw a rope up to Roma, she could slide down it and escape. How long a rope should I buy?

Longingly, Jules

_____

_____

_____

_____

2. Dear Pythagoras: Jack and I have a date. Our meeting spot is 120 miles directly west of Jack's home. Jack will ride his bicycle, and since the trip is all downhill, he should average about 30 miles per hour. I live 160 miles directly south of Jack, and I plan to drive. Suppose that Jack and I both leave home at the same time. What should be my average speed so that we will arrive at the meeting spot at the same time?

Promptly, Jill

_____

_____

_____

_____

3. Dear Pythagoras: My friend Jules told me that you help out with moat-rescue problems. Well, I've got one. The situation is this: My girlfriend's window is 15 feet above a moat that is 11 feet wide. I have a ladder that is 18 feet long. Can I rescue her, or should I buy a longer ladder?

Rung out, Igor

_____

_____

_____

1. Simplify the following expressions by combining like terms.

   a. $4x + 3x =$ _____

   b. $3x + 7 + x =$ _____

   c. $4 * (x + 2) + 2x - 6 =$ _____

   d. $(x + 3) * 2 - 2x =$ _____

2. Cindy simplified the expression $8(x + 10)$ as $(8 * x) + 10$. What did she do wrong? Explain her mistake and show how she should have solved the problem.

   _____

   _____

   _____

3. Solve each equation.

   a. $3x - 4 = 4x + 6$ _____

   b. $5 * (2 - 6) = 4g$ _____

   c. $3(2y - 3) = 15$ _____

   d. $\frac{(2x - 1)}{3} = 9$ _____

4. The perimeter of Triangle *ABC* is 18 inches. What is the length of each of its sides?

   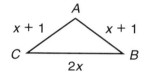

   Length of $\overline{AB}$ _____ Length of $\overline{BC}$ _____ Length of $\overline{AC}$ _____

5. The perimeter of Right Triangle *GLD* is 12 centimeters.

   What is the area of the triangle? _____

   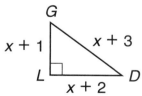

6. Jim often walks to school along Main Street and Elm Street. If he were to take Pythagoras Avenue instead, how many fewer blocks would he walk? _____

   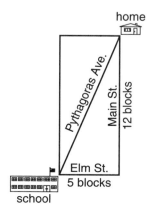

Unit 10: Geometry Topics

Unit 10 includes a variety of activities involving some of the more recreational, artistic, and lesser-known aspects of geometry. In *Fifth Grade Everyday Mathematics*, your child explored same-tile **tessellations.** A tessellation is an arrangement of closed shapes that covers a surface completely, without gaps or overlaps. Your kitchen or bathroom floor may be an example of a tessellation. A regular tessellation involves only one kind of regular polygon. Three examples are shown at the right.

In Unit 10 of *Sixth Grade Everyday Mathematics*, your child will explore semiregular tessellations. A **semiregular tessellation** is made from two or more kinds of regular polygons. For example, a semiregular tessellation can be made from equilateral triangles and squares.

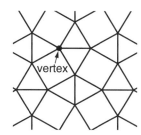

The angles around every vertex point in a semiregular tessellation must be congruent to the angles around every other vertex point. Notice that at each vertex point in the tessellation above, there are the vertices of 3 equilateral triangles and 2 squares, always in the same order.

The artist M. C. Escher used **transformation geometry**—translations, reflections, and rotations of geometric figures—to create intriguing tessellation art. Ask your child to show you the translation tessellation created in the style of Escher that the students will make in class.

Your child will also explore topology. **Topology**, sometimes called "rubber-sheet geometry," is a modern branch of geometry that deals with, among other topics, properties of geometric objects that do not change when the objects' shapes are changed. Ask your child to share with you some of the amazing ideas from topology, such as Möbius strips.

Finally, your child will explore cross sections of geometric solids. For example, if a cylinder is sliced as illustrated at the right, the resulting cross section will be a rectangle.

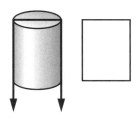

Some people easily visualize cross sections; others find it difficult. The introductory activities in Unit 10 provide students with the opportunity to make hypotheses about cross sections and then, using clay, to test their hypotheses.

Please keep this Family Letter for reference as your child works through Unit 10.

Math Tools

Your child will use the **Geometry Template** to explore and design tessellations. This tool includes a greater variety of shapes than on the pattern-block template from earlier grades. It might more specifically be called a *geometry and measurement template*. The measuring devices include inch and centimeter scales; a Percent Circle useful for making circle graphs; and both a full-circle and half-circle protractor.

Vocabulary

Important terms in Unit 10:

cross section A shape formed by the intersection of a plane and a geometric solid.

regular polygon A polygon whose sides are all the same length and whose angles are all equal.

rotation symmetry A figure has rotation symmetry if it can be rotated less than a full turn around a point or an axis so that the resulting figure (the *image*) exactly matches the original figure (the *preimage*).

tessellation An arrangement of shapes that covers a surface completely without overlaps or gaps. Also called a *tiling*.

topologically equivalent In *topology*, a term for shapes that can be transformed into each other by a topological transformation.

topological transformation A shrinking, stretching, twisting, bending, or other operation that doesn't change which points are next to each other in a shape.

topology The study of the properties of shapes which are unchanged by shrinking, stretching, twisting, bending, and similar transformations. (Tearing, breaking, and "sticking together," however, are not allowed.)

vertex point A point where corners of shapes in a *tessellation* meet. See also *tessellation*.

Use with Lesson 9.14

Do-Anytime Activities

To work with your child on the concepts taught in this unit, try these interesting and rewarding activities:

1 Familiarize yourself with the definition of *tessellation* (on previous page). Encourage your child to find tessellations in your home. Look in floor tile patterns, wallpaper patterns, and wall tile patterns. Have your child identify the shapes that make up the pattern.

2 If your child helps make dinner, you might begin a conversation about cross sections of vegetables. Ask your child as he or she is cutting to name the plane figure that the cross section shows. For example, if he or she is cutting carrots, your child might name circles. Then challenge him or her to change the position of the knife to obtain oval cross sections, triangle cross sections, and so on.

3 If you have an art program on your home computer, allow your child the time to experiment with computer graphic tessellations. Encourage him or her to share the creations with the class.

As You Help Your Child with Homework

As your child brings assignments home, you may want to go over the instructions together, clarifying them as necessary. The answers listed below will guide you through this unit's Study Links.

Study Link 10.1

1. Sample answer: A shape tessellates if it can be used to cover a surface without overlapping and without gaps between shapes.

3. Sample answer: In creating designs for tile patterns, wallpaper, and other household decorative and/or useful materials. Industrial designers might use tessellations to create waterproof surfaces.

Study Link 10.2

1.

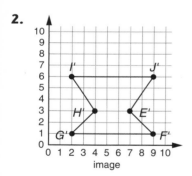

2.

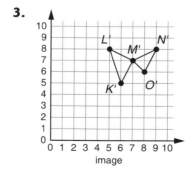

3.

Study Link 10.3

1. Order of rotation symmetry: 2

2. Order of rotation symmetry: 1

3. Order of rotation symmetry: 4

4. Order of rotation symmetry: 6

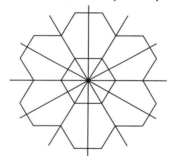

5. Order of rotation symmetry: 2

6. Order of rotation symmetry: infinite

Study Link 10.4

2. Sample answer: I was able to do this trick by folding the paper in half, placing the quarter in the fold, and then bending the paper upward as I gripped it at the outer edges of the crease.

Study Link 10.6 Sample answers:

1. The paper clips are linked to one another.

2. The paper clips and the rubber band are linked.

3. All of the paper clips are linked.

Use with Lesson 9.14.

Tessellation Exploration

1. Explain how you know whether a shape tessellates.

_____

_____

_____

_____

_____

_____

2. In your home, find an object that has a shape that tessellates.
   Trace the object several times below to show that it tessellates.

3. Explain why it might be useful to know which shapes tessellate.
   In which situations might you use tessellating shapes?

_____

_____

_____

_____

_____

Translations

Plot and label the vertices of the image that would result from each translation. One vertex of each image has already been plotted and labeled.

1.

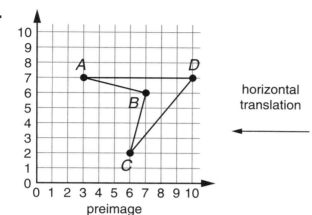

horizontal translation

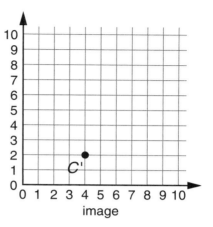

2.

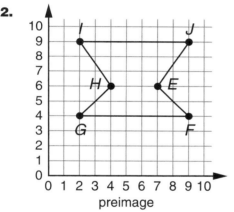

vertical translation

3.

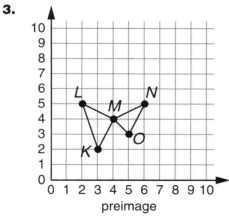

diagonal translation

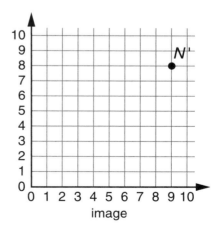

Rotation Symmetry

For each figure, draw the line(s) of reflection symmetry, if any.
Then determine the order of rotation symmetry for the figure.

1.

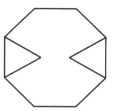

Order of rotation symmetry _____

2.

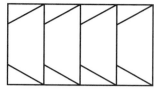

Order of rotation symmetry _____

3.

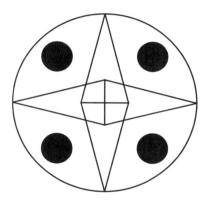

Order of rotation symmetry _____

4.

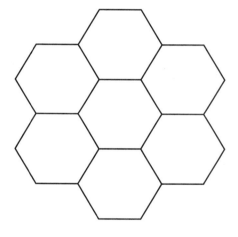

Order of rotation symmetry _____

5.

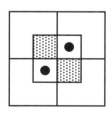

Order of rotation symmetry _____

6.

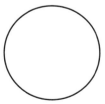

Order of rotation symmetry _____

Shrinking Quarter

1. Cut out the circle in the center of this page. It is about the size of a dime. Try to slip a quarter through the hole left in the page without tearing the paper.

2. Were you able to do this trick? If you were, explain how you did it. If not, explain why you were not able to.

_____

_____

_____

_____

_____

_____

A Topology Trick

Follow the procedure described below to tie a knot in a piece of string without letting go of the ends.

Step 1 Place a piece of string in front of you on a table or a desk.

Step 2 Fold your arms across your chest.

Step 3 With your arms still folded, grab the left end of the string with your right hand and the right end of the string with your left hand.

Step 4 Hold the ends of the string and unfold your arms. The string should now have a knot in it.

This trick works because of a principle in topology called **transference of curves.** Your arms had a knot in them before you picked up the string. When you unfolded your arms, you transferred the knot from your arms to the string.

Another Topology Trick

Follow the procedure described below to perform another topology trick that
works because of transference of curves.

Step 1 Gather the following materials: 2 to 8 large paper clips,
a strip of paper $1\frac{1}{2}$-by-11 inches; and a rubber band.

Step 2 Curve the strip of paper into an S-shape.
Attach two paper clips as shown at the right.

Step 3 Straighten the paper by holding
the ends and pulling sharply.

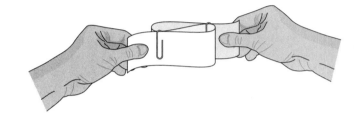

1. Describe your results.

_____

_____

2. Add a rubber band as shown.
Straighten the paper.

Describe your results.

_____

_____

3. Try including a chain of paper clips as shown.

Describe your results.

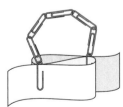

_____

_____

Family Letter

Congratulations!

By completing *Sixth Grade Everyday Mathematics,* your child has accomplished a great deal. Thank you for all of your support.

This Family Letter is intended as a resource for you to use throughout your child's vacation. It includes an extended list of Do-Anytime Activities, directions for games that can be played at home, a list of mathematics-related books to get from your library, and a sneak preview of what your child might be learning in seventh grade. Enjoy your vacation!

Do-Anytime Activities

Mathematics means more when it is rooted in real-life situations. To help your child review many of the concepts that he or she has learned in sixth grade, we suggest the following activities for you and your child to do together over vacation. These activities will help your child build on the skills that your child has learned this year and help prepare him or her for a seventh grade mathematics course.

1 Practice quick recall of multiplication facts. Include "extended facts," such as $70 * 8 = 560$ and $70 * 80 = 5,600$.

2 Practice calculating with percents. Use a variety of contexts, such as sales tax, discounts, and sports performances.

3 Use measuring devices—rulers, metersticks, yardsticks, tape measures, thermometers, scales, and so on. Measure in both U.S. customary and metric units.

4 Estimate the answers to calculations, such as the bill at a restaurant or store, the distance to a particular place, the number of people at an event, and so on.

5 Play games like those in the *Student Reference Book.*

Building Skills through Games

The following section lists rules for games that can be played at home. The number cards used in some games can be made from 3"-by-5" index cards.

Name That Number

Materials   4 each of number cards 0 through 10, and
1 each of number cards 11 through 20

Players   2 or 3

Object of the game To collect the most cards

Directions

1. Shuffle the cards and deal five cards to each player. Place the remaining cards number-side down. Turn over the top card and place it beside the deck. This is the **target number** for the round.

2. Players try to match the target number by adding, subtracting, multiplying, or dividing the numbers on as many of their cards as possible. A card may only be used once.

3. Players write their solutions on a sheet of paper. When players have written their best solutions, they do the following:

   · Set aside the cards they used to name the target number.

   · Replace them by drawing new cards from the top of the deck.

   · Put the old target number on the bottom of the deck.

   · Turn over a new target number and play another hand.

4. Play continues until there are not enough cards left to replace all of the players' cards. The player who sets aside more cards wins the game.

Use with Lesson 10.7.

Fraction Action, Fraction Friction

Materials
- ❏ One set of 16 *Fraction Action, Fraction Friction* cards. The card set includes a card for each of the following fractions (for several fractions there are 2 cards):

$$\frac{1}{2}, \frac{1}{3}, \frac{2}{3}, \frac{1}{4}, \frac{3}{4}, \frac{1}{6}, \frac{1}{6}, \frac{5}{6}, \frac{1}{12}, \frac{1}{12}, \frac{5}{12}, \frac{5}{12}, \frac{7}{12}, \frac{7}{12}, \frac{11}{12}, \frac{11}{12}.$$

- ❏ One or more calculators

Players   2 or 3

Object of the game   To gather a set of fraction cards with a sum as close as possible to 2, without going over 2.

Directions

1. Shuffle the deck. Place the pile facedown between the players.

2. Players take turns.

   · On each player's first turn, he or she takes a card from the top of the pile, then places it faceup on the playing surface.

   · On each of the player's following turns, he or she announces one of the following:

   "Action"   This means that the player wants an additional card. The player believes that the sum of the cards is not close enough to 2 to win the hand. The player thinks that another card will bring the sum of the cards closer to 2, without going over 2.

   "Friction"   This means that the player does not want an additional card. The player believes that the sum of the cards is close enough to 2 to win the hand. The player thinks there is a good chance that taking another card will make the sum of the cards greater than 2.

   Once a player says "Friction," he or she cannot say "Action" on any turn after that.

3. Play continues until all players have announced "Friction" or have a set of cards whose sum is greater than 2. The player whose sum is closest to 2 without going over 2 is the winner of the hand. Players may check one another's sums with their calculators.

4. Reshuffle the cards and begin again. The winner of the game is the first player to win five hands.

Use with Lesson 10.7.

Vacation Reading with a Mathematical Twist

Books can contribute to student learning by presenting mathematics in a combination of real-world and imaginary contexts. The titles listed below were recommended by teachers who use *Everyday Mathematics* in their classrooms.

You might want to invest in a book of problem-solving activities. Here are a few suggestions:

The Book of Think by Marilyn Burns. Little, Brown and Company, 1976.

The I Hate Mathematics! Book by Marilyn Burns. Little, Brown and Company, 1975.

Math for Smarty Pants by Marilyn Burns. Little, Brown and Company, 1982.

Math Logic Puzzles by Kurt Smith. Sterling Publishing Co., Inc., 1996.

The following are books with more recreational themes:

Kids' Book of Secret Codes, Signals, and Ciphers by E. A. Grant. Running Press, 1989.

Mathemagic by Raymond Blum. Sterling Publishing Co., Inc., 1992.

Math Tricks, Puzzles, and Games by Raymond Blum. Sterling Publishing Co., Inc., 1995.

The Seasons Sewn: A Year in Patchwork by Ann Whitford Paul. Browndeer Press, 1996.

Looking Ahead: Seventh Grade

Next year, your child will

- increase skills with percents, decimals, and fractions.
- compute with fractions, decimals, and positive and negative numbers.
- continue to write algebraic expressions for simple situations.
- solve equations.
- use formulas to solve problems.

Again, thank you for all of your support this year. Have fun continuing your child's mathematical experiences throughout the vacation!

Best wishes for an enjoyable vacation.

Use with Lesson 10.7.